The Betrayal of Wisdom

The Betrayal of Wisdom

&

The Challenge To Philosophy Today

Robert J. Kreyche

Professor of Philosophy
University of Arizona
(Tucson)

alba house

A DIVISION OF THE SOCIETY OF ST. PAUL
STATEN ISLAND, NEW YORK 10314

Library of Congress Cataloging in Publication Data

Kreyche, Robert J 1920-
   The betrayal of wisdom.

    Bibliography: p.
    1. Man. 2. Philosophy, Modern. 3. Civilization, Modern--1950-
4. Empiricism. I. Title.
BD450.K695   190   72-304
ISBN 0-8189-0248-5

Designed, printed and bound by the Fathers and Brothers of the
Society of St. Paul as part of their communications apostolate.

Copyright 1972 by the Society of St. Paul,
2187 Victory Blvd., Staten Island, N. Y. 10314.

Ad Patrem et Amicum,
Edward J. Edwards,
Cujus Auxilio Haec Verba
In Verbo
Fundentur

THE PRESENT VOL-
ume is a modest attempt to restore philosophy to its rightful
place in society. To say nothing of the view that "the common man" has of philosophy, philosophers themselves have
largely lost sight of the meaning of their vocation. It is not
simply a question of a "bad press," but of a lack of confidence
on the part of philosophers to re-develop and re-create a wisdom tradition for their times. Some persons have said that
philosophy, like God, is dead. Personally, I feel they are
wrong. But there is a problem of explaining the *alleged* death
of philosophy to those who hardly know it exists.

No doubt philosophy—aged discipline that it is—has been
subjected to many a crisis. But I myself would refuse to
accept the demise of philosophy at the time of its greatest
need, which is to say, that the purpose of this volume is,
not to revive a dead corpse (a futile task in any case), but
to help pave the way toward some new paths of creativity
in an area of knowledge that is in need of fresh life, impetus, and growth.

This book is based on a number of convictions, but
among them the very important one that each generation
must "fight" for the truth, not simply in the sense of defend-
ing it, but in the sense of struggling to find out for itself
where the truth of things lies. Apropos, then, of the needs
of our times, it is not enough merely to revive idealism,
pragmatism, or any other "ism" with the thought in mind
that such a philosophy, as ready-made package, *may* be

relevant to our times. One must rather live through, indeed, *suffer out* the way of truth as he sees it for his own times and in light of his own experience and needs.

In his famous work, entitled *A Study of History*, Arnold Toynbee has spoken of the "savior with the time-machine," the sort of person who attempts to solve present problems by an eclectic reversion to the past. In agreement with Toynbee I feel that all such attempts are futile since the past is irreversible and since each generation must carve out for itself a new path. Such, then, is the challenge, for philosophy, namely, to realize that philosophy is no more dead nor alive than philosophers make it out to be. If, indeed, they do escape *as philosophers* from the real conflicts of life, then that is their prerogative, yet in so doing they should be prepared to suffer the loss of their good reputation. On the other hand, if philosophers can show that their own brand of wisdom has a deep-seated meaning for our times, then sooner or later the world will regain its respect for philosophy, and in so doing be enabled to see it in a fresh light.

In any event I am hardly persuaded that the wellsprings of philosophy have been drained dry for all time to come. Neither Descartes, Hume, Kant, nor any other genius of the past has had the last word. There comes a time when one should not merely canonize the geniuses of the past, but inspire new ones to develop their own inner vision of the truth. To this end I have attempted to do my part to regain for philosophy a confidence that has been lost, and if in the end my own modest effort has served to mark the return of "Sophia," which is simply the Greek name for "Wisdom," I shall be happy that the message of this book shall not have fallen on deaf ears.

One of the needs of today, then, is to develop a philosophy with a new sense of direction and one which, given the nature of man as it *is*, can develop some new categories that will satisfy some of the legitimate cravings of the contemporary mind. Among these cravings I detect the need for a philosophy that will give fuller and more mature expression to the dimension of the personal in human affairs, to the value and importance of religious experience and all that it conveys, and to the outgoing movements of love for our fellowman as a member of a race (the *human* race) that yet needs to be more closely united.

Too, these legitimate cravings need to be inserted within the yet larger context of a new approach both to psychology and metaphysics which I call "integral realism" and a "radical empiricism of the spirit." In general, philosophy is still too much riddled with the inauthentic modes both of rationalism and empiricism to have paved the way toward a new type of synthesis that may yet both *re*-humanize philosophy itself and give it the vitality it needs. Such a synthesis is possible, and I have even tried to indicate the direction it might take, but whether or not it will be effected depends largely on how many philosophers will devote themselves to the task.

Further, it remains to be seen whether a new synthesis, if it is forthcoming, will proceed from academic quarters or not. As most of us know, many of the world's great philosophers were not academicians at all, and Schopenhauer went so far as to boast that his love for philosophy was too great for him to become a professor of it. But this is no matter of concern—as long as the development takes place. For myself, I shall be content like Locke to serve as an under-laborer who is willing to till the soil in the hope that others will use that soil as a source of further creativity. Since this book (relatively short as it is) has been six years in the making, a variety of influences have led to its development in its present form. One of them was the gracious invitation given me by Dr. Robert M. Hutchins to present my views at *The Center For The Study of Democratic Institutions* in Montecito, California under the topic of "The Practical Task of Philosophy Today." From the challenge of that talk I developed some of the highlights of Chapter 13 which sums up some of the central themes and concerns of this book.

As to other sources of indebtedness I wish to express thanks to the Graduate School and Alumni Organization of the University of Arizona for supplementary grants that assisted me in the development of this work. Too, I am especially grateful to Mr. George Godas who, as my research assistant, has offered valuable suggestions in one of the central revisions of the text, and to the secretaries of the philosophy department for their competent clerical help. Finally, I am indebted to my wife, Ann, for the encouragement she gave me in bringing this manuscript to its state of completion.

MAY, 1972

Robert J. Kreyche

CONTENTS

The Betrayal of Wisdom

INTRO-
DUCTION

IN THE PAST few years no small amount of attention has been directed on all levels, including the level of our popular magazines, to the vast amount of confusion that exists in the modern world. This confusion manifests itself in a thousand ways, but most especially in the doubt that has been raised concerning the very possibility of man's coming to the truth about himself, the world, and God, assuming, as many persons today do not, that God exists.

As a professor of philosophy I willingly share the burden of responsibility for this state of confusion since philosophers generally are as guilty of producing it as any other class of men. Yet in sharing this burden I feel a particular sense of urgency (in the writing of another book) not to heighten the confusion, but to diminish it, and if possible, to provide some insights for the reader that may help to light up a new path.

Though this volume embraces a variety of topics, I have restricted myself to a few basic themes. Among these themes are such items as the need for a proper diagnosis of the decline of philosophy in our times, and more positively the need for a new empiricism. I shall try to show also that one of the most profound needs of our times is not the multiplication of theories, but the return to philosophy as therapy— as a kind of healing for the diseases of the mind. Too, throughout this volume I shall be initiating the development of a position which I call "integral realism"—as a method of synthesizing the various elements of truth that have been disjoined for hundreds of years. In a word, I shall attempt to restore confidence in the natural realism of the mind, a confidence that has been lost under the overpowering impact of scepticism, positivism, and agnosticism.

The central thesis of this book is to point up the *need* (in a sense not intended by John Dewey) *of a reconstruction in philosophy* of the sort that will help modern man to extricate himself from the morass into which he has sunk. This is not a task, however, which I expect single-handedly to accomplish on my own. My personal task is to perform a kind of diagnosis in philosophical terms of the disease, indeed, of the diseases, of the modern mind, and secondly, to provide some few of the remedies for its restoration to a condition of good health.

Good *mental* health is not simply a state of mind that enables an individual person "to get along" with the ordinary problems of his day-to-day environment. More profoundly it is a condition of life whereby an individual or society at large is able to cope with the larger problems that lie at the basis of one's ordinary affairs. In the sense in which I use "mental health" I would judge that many persons who seem to be well-adjusted are lacking in it, if only for want of some kind of ultimate goal.

In my personal work with students over the past twenty-five years, if there is any one factor that shines out above all the rest, it is the deep-seated desire in their lives to serve some goal or plan that is larger than themselves. The problem with these students, as with society at large, is that of their discontent, conscious or otherwise, with the purely pragmatic goals of the past. What young people are seeking today is a set of ideals that will imprint the stamp of personal meaning on their lives, and instinctively they turn

4

to philosophy as a symbol of their goals and ideals.

We have now reached a stage in our history when we can no longer pretend that ultimate problems are matters of only secondary concern. The youth of today especially are surfeited with any and all attempts, however contrived, to pretend that the trivialities of life, modern life in particular, are the only things that matter, as though by a technique of distraction we could make our existential neuroses disappear. They have come into possession of a truth, often closed to the minds of their elders, that any attempt to uphold the dream world of Mr. Babbitt is to play a losing game.

Let us not therefore suppose that the role of philosophy is to treat ultimate questions *as if* they did not exist. These questions do exist in the very "gut" of our being, and because they do it is important to bridge the gap between philosophy and life. Yet in spite of this need there is no greater evil to some persons' minds than that of "dogmatism" in philosophy—of the sort that prefers to know *something* of the relation between philosophy and life. The question we must raise, then, is this: Do not the *methodological* dogmatists take a yet more "extreme" position in their refusal to allow any pre-commitment to a goal? I am, of course, in fundamental agreement with those neo-socratics who insist on the openness of philosophy to search out new answers for old questions. I disagree, however, with the contention that the sole value of philosophy is the *search* for these answers, and not the answers themselves, and if the latter is not the case then truly philosophy is nothing more than a game.

This entire volume is a defense of the position that philosophy is an earnest inquiry into the serious questions of life. It is not a game nor a sophisticated past-time, but man's highest endeavor to solve these problems. Science does not

5

have the answers to these problems, nor does education, politics, or law. But the role of philosophy as wisdom is precisely to conduct such a search in the hope that some of the answers can be found.

To assume that philosophy is something more than abstract, analytical inquiry into questions of trivial concern is to imply the fundamental validity of the idea initiated perhaps by the pythagoreans and the stoics that philosophy is essentially related to the problems of human life. This is to say that the work of philosophy is just as truly synthetic as it is analytic—synthetic, not in the sense of arbitrary system-building, but in the sense of trying to provide an integrated approach to life-problems. Certainly William James (1842-1910) was no rationalist insofar as his brand of radical pluralism forbade any type of system-building in the Hegelian sense of the word; yet, as a matter of fact, it was James who gave this admirable definition of truth as that *which ultimately integrates our lives*.

To the extent, then, that philosophy performs such a task, it comes to grips with the essential problems of life and happily loses the title of being something "purely academic." The "purely academic" in the pejorative sense of the word is the kind of knowledge that divorces itself from life-problems, and my central thesis is that philosophy least of all can afford to create such a divorce, such a split.

No doubt there have been many reasons—some of them historical—why philosophy has become in recent times a highly specialized game in the hands of linguistic technicians and there is every reason to think that the "quest for certainty" can at times produce ambiguous results. Yet in the opinion of this author philosophers have become paralyzed by an excessive fear that anything short of a mathematical certainty in the area of philosophy has absolutely no value

Introduction

at all. What they forget is Aristotle's wise advice that one should not seek for greater certainty in any area of inquiry than the nature of the subject allows.

Be all of this as it may, we shall get on with the task of trying to discover whether philosophy is in a coma or not, and if so, whether it is worth our task to revive it and in what sense. To some persons, including myself, the apparent "death" of philosophy represents only a stage preliminary to its rebirth in a different form. Whatever the case may be, we should have to agree that philosophy is in a moribund state if it has no place to reside other than in the craters of scepticism. If, on the other hand, the return and re-development of a realistic philosophy remains a permanent possibility, it is quite possible for philosophy to mark out a new path.

1

━━━━━━━━━━━━━━━━━━━━━━━━━━━━━━━━━━

WHICH
WAY
WISDOM?

Introductory
Remarks

A LONG TIME
ago I had read something in Etienne Gilson's (1884-   )
Being and Some Philosophers to the effect that one cannot,
after all, say everything at once, but only in gradual stages,
and so it is with the philosopher: his message (if indeed he
has one) is something that will come upon him only over a
period of years, but sooner or later it will out, and when it
does it is hard to know (as it was with Parmenides) where
to begin and where to end. Yet in a very real sense it makes
little difference where to begin or end provided one follows
the path of wisdom as *he* (the philosopher) sees it, intimately, and as part of his own experience, and not in slavish
imitation of somebody else.

Accordingly I need not apologize to the reader for the
personal slant of this volume, as I am far more concerned
with insight, both in Bernard Lonergan's (1904-   ) sense
and my own, than with any formal syllogistic proof. Further,
the notion of philosophy as "science," even in the classical
sense of the term, might well give ground to the notion of
philosophy as wisdom—and that in a deeply personal key. As
a philosopher friend once remarked to me, "Let's no longer
worry about 'right' and 'wrong' statements in philosophy—

only about 'wise' and 'foolish' ones." I will not dwell, of course, on the many foolish statements that have been made by philosophers over the years except to recall Bertrand Russell's remark that there is no bit of nonsense that was not professed at one time or another by some philosopher. But getting back to my friend's statement, the more I think about it the more am I convinced of its depth: Truth is something dynamic, something that grows and develops, and when it does reach its point of fruition it is no longer mere knowledge, but "wisdom," and it is the practical pursuit of wisdom in the affairs of contemporary life that is the focal point of this book.[1]

The Mystery of Existence and the Needs of Contemporary Man

Long before existentialism had become a byword—both among philosophers and the public at large—I had read as an undergraduate in college a challenging little volume by Jacques Maritain (1882-   ) under the intriguing title *Existence and The Existent*. Though the book itself made a profound impression on my mind, what impressed me most of all was its title. Should not philosophy, after all, concern itself first and foremost with the problem, indeed, with the *mystery* of human existence? And is it not wrong for philosophers of whatever persuasion—in the face of the realities

---

1. Personally, I have always felt deeply in my bones that there was something inauthentic about being a part-time philosopher as though one could at certain moments in one's life don the philosopher's robe, and at certain other moments go on as if philosophy had nothing to do with life. The fact of the matter is, speaking for myself at least, that philosophy is nothing unless it is a reflection on life, an outgrowth of one's personal experience.

I am in full agreement

of life—to withdraw into a make-believe world of their own? Much to the chagrin perhaps of many a professional philosopher, I have always felt that philosophy should serve people's needs, not in the same way, of course, as science, medicine, or technology, but in a way that gets to the bottom of things, to the subconscious needs of the spirit.[2] To me it is a remarkable thing, as far as philosophers are concerned, that the public should be ever damned. No doubt they have felt, many of them, that philosophy is so highly specialized a discipline that any attempt to communicate with the public at large would fall on deaf ears.

Personally, I do not share such a view.[3] It is my own conviction that there is something of a philosopher in every man who is willing to take the trouble to reflect on his own experience, and I have often found an almost reverential awe of philosophy in some untutored souls whose instincts told them (as the instincts of some professional philosophers do not) that philosophy is a kind of wisdom that is worthy at all costs to be searched out and found.

It is extremely important at this particular moment of history for philosophers to re-awaken from their non-existential slumbers and to re-discover the fact that they too are men of flesh and blood whose primary concern should be to communicate, not anemically, but passionately with other men of flesh and blood who are crying out, both inside the walls of our universities and without, for wisdom, and the

---

2. Philosophy therefore, far from being, as it so often is, a method of escape from reality, should be above all else an unremitting search for the real, the existent, the authentic.

3. Especially in view of the fact that the public is getting more sophisticated each day. Old style methods of oratory and rhetoric are no longer adequate as a means of communication, and the younger generation especially is dead serious in its attempt to know what philosophers call the "ultimate truth of things."

kind of knowledge that gets beyond the trivialities of modern life.

The great need today, when everyone else has given himself over to some narrow field of specialization, is the revival of the philosophy, not of mind, but of *spirit*. We have had too much philosophy of mind, divorced from the roots of a deep inner experience, an anemic mind, that mistakingly separates itself from the life of the spirit. Perhaps the German word "Geist" most adequately conveys the approach I am trying to suggest, an approach that represents a radical departure from the rationalism of the last three or four hundred years.

Rationalism in philosophy means that you recognize only the conscious level of existence which is the level of images, thoughts, ideas, or what have you. It denies that there is anything else like the iceberg that lies underneath. By contrast a true philosophy of the spirit, or better yet, of *integral man*,[4] is a recognition of the whole vast realm of human emotions, of the needs of the spirit, of the inner conflicts that lie within the soul. Such an approach to philosophy is not psychology, but a true *meta*-psychology insofar as it is an attempt to get beyond the "empirical" in the narrow, confining sense of a purely specialized technique. Thus understood, philosophy bases itself on a recognition of the realities of the "heart" as well as those of the head, of the emotions as well as the mind, of the unconscious as well as the conscious, of man as a total being of body and spirit, and neither body nor spirit alone.

If in the course of this volume I emphasize the needs of the "soul" or those of the "spirit" I do not wish the reader

4. Later we shall have much to say about "integral realism" as a method which endeavors to synthesize those elements of human experience that have been separated and distorted for the past few hundred years.

to think that I am lapsing into one of the "spiritualisms" of the past as it is my deepest conviction that man is a creature of flesh, blood, and bones. On the other hand, the meta-psychology of which I speak is an approach to the problem of man that goes directly opposite to the notion of man as "organism," as a bodily organism alone. My central concern is to deal with man in his subconscious depths and in terms of his most deep-rooted needs. Above all else, I am concerned with the problem of self-transcendence—a self-transcendence that the behaviorist psychology of B. F. Skinner (1904-   ) and others denies.[5]

When I speak of the need of philosophy as wisdom, I am especially mindful of the fact that there is a singular absence in our universities today of any genuine philosophizing of the sort that bases itself on the real needs of the spirit. Philosophy itself has become a narrow form of specialization that artificially removes itself from the real conflicts of life and prefers instead to install itself in a comfortable and abstract realm of mathematical and logical truths. It is no longer a philosophy of existence, but of essence, considered apart from the real world in which men and women suffer, work and spend their lives. The tragedy of this situation is especially evident in today's youth, notably on our university campuses, who are searching for wisdom, but have no idea of where it is to be found.[6]

Which Is Primary—Method or Life-Truths?

Until now I have no more than hinted of the need, in a

5. See Chapter Eight on this subject, "The Primacy of Self-Transcendence."
6. What they want to know is how their philosophy professors think in their lives, and not merely in relation to their textbooks. What they are looking for is wisdom, not merely knowledge.

sense never intended by John Dewey (1859-1952), of a reconstruction in philosophy. As for the method of reconstruction prescribed by Dewey let it be said that the uncompromising biologism of his basic philosophical outlook was a factor which, though intendedly oriented toward the integration of philosophy and life, actually prevented him from the real accomplishment of his task. Thus although Dewey forever spoke of "felt needs" it was never of the needs of the *spirit* that he spoke, only those of the organism. To Dewey man himself was an organism, neither more nor less, whose intelligence was an instrument, not for grasping transcendental truths, but only for coping with the means for the advancement of biological goals.

While I therefore admire Dewey's attempt to integrate philosophy and life, his own approach to the problem was, in my view, a failure on three counts: (1) the limitations of his pragmatism prevented him from understanding the deeper and more radical needs of the spirit; (2) his view of the nature of man was too heavily dominated by a purely biologistic point of view; and (3) his stress on the "supremacy of method" subordinated the methods of philosophy to the methods of science as such, and it is on this question of method I should now like to dwell.

On one occasion I invited a professor of philosophy to give a talk to a class of mine on philosophy of education. The central point of his talk was that the sole concern of the philosopher should be in the area of "method." To him the important thing was not the "game" but the method that you used in "playing" it—as if in any case philosophy were merely a game. When I asked my guest whether the method should not adjust itself to the aims of inquiry and

14

not the other way around, his only response was that aims and goals can only be empirically discovered and not "superimposed." In spite of the irrelevancy of his answer I still wondered how it might be possible to pursue *any* method without some foreknowledge of the goals, a query to which no answer was forthcoming.

The above anecdote is to me a simple illustration of the fact that philosophers, as the one class of men who could and should become lovers of wisdom, have suffered a loss of nerve, not through a failure to give heed to the problem of method, but through a failure to give heed to anything else. The existential meaning and direction of philosophy as wisdom is a pursuit that has been all but abandoned, in favor of the view that philosophy is a kind of game. The exact nature of the game itself, whether it is a language game or a game dealing with the p's and q's of logic is no matter of great concern. What does matter, and the only thing that matters, is the logical observance of the rules.

In contrast, then, to the idea of philosophy as having to do with method alone I want to stress here the need for philosophy as coming to grips with the substantive truths of human life. In the Preface to one of my previous works, *God and Contemporary Man*, John Howard Griffin (1920-) made a classic remark as to the need for "de-ghetto-izing" philosophy. In his view and mine, philosophy has removed and isolated itself from the problems of ordinary men "forming as it were a virtual prison from which truth could not escape to inform the activities of man." There was a failure, in his words, "in clinging to a certain academic staleness out of fear that something was risked if the fresh air of new concepts were allowed in. What does philosophy, after all, have to do with man's daily existence?—with his shavings and his cooking and his loving and suffering and bringing children to light? At the practical level the two are hardly on speaking terms."[7]

Since the time these words were written the situation has in no way changed. Philosophy today is no more "empirical" in the sense of appealing to man's deepest needs, *including the needs of the spirit,* than it was at the time of Hume. Like David Hume (1711-1776), many philosophers today feel, in spite of their best intentions, a sort of compulsion to create schizophrenically a rift between their lives as ordinary human beings and their philosophic systems of thought.[8] They are uncompromising realists when they go shopping for groceries, but unmitigated sceptics when they don their philosopher's robe. For such philosophers it is seemingly impossible either in principle or practice to reconcile, to say nothing of integrating, philosophy with life. What is far less excusable, however, is the attempt to *justify* this self-imposed rupture between philosophy and life in the name of "empiricism"—an empiricism of the sort, let it be said, that is based on an anatomic dissection of experience rather than on any attempt to unify it from within. The mistake here is that of constructing a method that is *a priori* to the facts, and if it turns out that the facts do not fit the method, then so much the worse for the facts.

7. See **God and Contemporary Man** (Milwaukee: The Bruce Publishing Co., 1965), pp. IX-X of Preface.

8. It is not my intent to impugn the motives of either Hume or anyone else. As a matter of fact, the **motive** of Hume was the noble aim of developing a unified science of human nature even as his contemporaries in science were achieving a unified view of the physical world. The problem, however, with Hume, was his failure—due to a sensationalistic theory of knowledge—to take a close look at the integral nature of experience as seen in its subconscious depths.

16

Which Way Wisdom?

In a later chapter I shall write at greater length of the need for a new empiricism of the sort that does seek an integration between philosophy and life, but for now it is sufficient to make the point that there is a failure of nerve on the part of philosophers, given their diminished and restricted view of the nature of their vocation—to launch out into the deep. For one thing they have little or no ambition, in spite of the incessant cant of "empiricism," to create a a new path to learning without some kind of pre-commitment to a philosophical system of the past. To be a philosopher is almost by definition (in this mistaken view of things) to associate oneself with some thinker of the past and to elaborate *ad infinitum* on that tradition. At the time of their greatest challenge philosophers tend to look backward, not forward. They prefer to retreat into a finely spun elaboration of past systems rather than to create ideas of their own.[9]

Concluding Remark

In the chapters that follow I hope to show that the life of philosophy lies in the development of a creative minority who have the courage to see old truths in a new light—in the light of contemporary needs. Most especially, I have a desire to convey to the reader what my own perspective is in the area of "Lebensphilosophie," "philosophy of life." In a later chapter I want to open up a new vista of philosophy,

9. This appeal to creativity in no way implies a **carte blanche** rejection of what is valid in past systems of philosophy, as the only sensible way of philosophizing is to build on the basis of what is **true** within the traditional systems. My only point here is that of the futility of accepting past systems without re-thinking them in relation to the needs of the present. All philosophy should be a reflection both on past **and present** experience, be it that of the individual person or of mankind as a whole.

not merely as theory (since we have had a surfeit of "theories" over the last few hundred years), but of philosophy as a special kind of therapy for the needs of our times. This notion may not be altogether new, but it is one that has been seriously neglected. The fruitfulness of the idea of philosophy as therapy will, I trust, become increasingly evident to the reader as he enters more deeply into the spirit and intent of this book.

2

PHILOSOPHY
IN SEARCH
OF ITSELF

*Introductory
Remark*

IN THE PAST
chapter I have spoken of the need for an existential approach
to philosophy of the sort that secures an integration between
philosophy and life. At a time when philosophy appears to
be dead, I have tried to indicate that this is the moment
both of its greatest challenge and of its greatest need. What
I have advocated therefore is a less rigid confinement to the
problem of method as such and a re-awakening to the need
for a new philosophy of life.

But where shall we find it? Not certainly in an unending mentalistic pursuit of epistemological problems as such,
but rather in an understanding of man, and of man as he is in
the *totality* of his being—in his loves, hates, desires, hopes,
and joys. Human nature, being the complex thing that it is,
should be searched out in its multiple dimensions, and such
an approach means the abandonment of rationalism in all of
its forms, including the classical modern form whereby the
analytical intelligence of man is separated from the dynamism
of life. Realism, as I propose it in this book, is opposed to
subjectivism, but especially that form of it which upholds
the mind of man to be the ultimate measure of things. To
restore confidence in philosophy—the confidence it rightly

19

2

deserves—we must restore philosophy itself to a state of
health whereby the natural realism of the human intelligence
is again interrelated to the overall purpose of life, and this
means that philosophy can no longer remain in a prison
house of its own ideas.

Ciphers and Pointers

As we progress with the notion of truth (objective, philosophical truth) as a kind of therapy for the mind, we shall
see more intimately how philosophy is more needed today
than it was at any time previous. But this for a later development. What we need to know now is to find out what
philosophy is, and what it is not. Above all else, philosophy
is *not* a vacuum-packed system of self-contained truths. Descartes thought that such was the case, and so did Leibniz
and Wolff, but the essential fallacy in the thinking of all of
these men was the presupposition that the philosophical
mind could, as it were, contain, comprehensively so, the
mystery of all existence. Rationalism in all of its forms attempts to harness the fullness of reality in the limited categories of our own minds.

To counteract such a view let us here keep in mind that
truth, in whatever manner we come upon it, is never something that can literally be captured with a net, and on this
point William James has a powerful insight. According to
him our knowledge of the truth is always a relative knowledge.[1] It is knowledge whereby we come to know things

1. "Relative" in the sense of "limited," "imperfect," "finite," but not
in the sense of a total variance from one individual to another, as it is
precisely my position to state that we can and do have an **objective**
knowledge of truth in all of its variant forms.

20

only in glimpses like a bird on the wing. Let us say then that truth is too dynamic a thing to allow us to submit it to an unending process of dissection and hyper-analysis. Like an organism it is best appreciated in its natural setting rather than in a condition of having been deflowered, anatomized, classified and examined as a "scientific" specimen.

Later I shall speak more generally of the contribution of existentialism to the development of a life-philosophy, but in this present context I want to call to mind Karl Jaspers' (1883-1969) notion of our approach to reality through ciphers and pointers. According to him "reality" is not, as it were, something open for our inspection so as to be seen all at once. Although reality does call for openness *on our part*, the nature of the real is such that ordinarily it is hidden from our eyes. The limits therefore of our knowledge are clearly marked off by the fact that we can only have *intimations* of the real in periodic moments of crisis. It is at such times as these that we discern, however delicately and inarticulately so, the symptomatic expression of the real through "ciphers." These latter provide no more than a hint of the deeper levels of existence—for those who have pre-pared themselves to read between the lines.

In sharp contrast to a view such as this we are con-fronted with the inherent fallacy of all rationalistic systems of thought which presuppose, however obliquely so, that the ultimate "function" of mind is, as it were, to "dominate" reality, to "control" it, to subject it to the exigencies of its own arbitrary laws and in so doing, to create what Dewey has aptly described as a "wholesale" type of philosophy.

Knowledge and Understanding

Philosophy, as I see it, is far less a matter of *control* (and here the pragmatists keep company with the rationalists) than it is of an authentic *understanding* of the real.[2] But by "understanding" here I do not mean mere knowledge as a purely detached and objective sort of thing. I mean "understanding" literally in the sense in which it can be acquired only as the result of a certain connaturality with the "object" and as something one acquires out of a motive of love. To catch the full weight of my meaning I must ask the reader to consider the difference between merely "knowing" a person and "understanding" him. Mere knowledge of a person means that you know his name, or occupation, or address, or even that he plays tennis, or likes Beethoven. Knowledge of this sort is nothing more than knowledge *about*, and in this sense many persons "know" philosophy. They might even be experts in the mechanism of ideas and their consequences—dilettantes, if you will, or even intellectual tiros. Such knowledge, however, is not philosophy, nor does it lead the way to truth in the deeper sense of an integral realism as I shall later explain this term.

By contrast, then, what do you mean when you say that you "understand" a person like understanding your wife or your mother or your child? Clearly that you know something about that person in depth and as an outgrowth of your personal love. When you say, therefore, that you *understand* a person, you mean first of all that you accept that person for what he or she is; you do not use that person as an object, as a toy, or as a tool of your own selfish pleasures and desires. Understanding here is not simply a question of respect but of sympathy and love. It is the result of a

---

2. Recall here Francis Bacon's (1561-1626) short-sighted dictum that knowledge is power. Applied to problems of technology it is certainly that, but much more: Knowledge, even on the level of science, must be **understanding** before it is power and control.

22

willingness to share and to sacrifice, to put up with all sorts of contradictions for the one you love. It is a predisposition to judge a person (whenever the need arises) in a favorable light.

Let the reader decide for himself what it fully means to understand a person rather than merely to know him. My own concern at the moment is to show that the philosopher who is truly such is not scandalized by the fact that reality is something far in excess of his own limited capacity to know it. Instead he is quite willing to accept the limitations of his mind and to embrace reality as he finds it, in all of its richness, diversity, and strength. He discovers too that "truth" is neither a phantom nor a hypostatized essence— dwelling as it were in a heaven of its own—but something quite real and substantial that comes to one piecemeal and as the result of a painstaking search.

But the essential point here is that philosophy is, above all else, what I call *intellectus vitae*—understanding of life. Between the realm of pure mystical intuition (which lies beyond the reach of ordinary men) and the realm of a purely rational discourse (which tends to become too mechanical like the making of syllogisms) there is a manner of knowing that seems eminently suited, not merely to the mind as such, but to man as a total entity. It is a way of knowing that is more than mere knowledge because it involves a sympathetic and connatural interest in persons and things for what they are in themselves, and not as we reconstruct them according to our own ends, purposes and desires.

Wisdom in this sense, as understanding of life, is something which is accessible to all who are willing to cultivate it, but alas, everything in our culture seems to block the way toward the restoration of philosophy understood in this light. No need, however, for pessimism as long as we can keep the ideal alive, and the ideal in question is that of an enlarged empiricism that will serve to open up whole new vistas of truth to those who are willing to cast off the shackles of subjectivism. What I want most of all is to inspire in my reader a strong personal confidence in the native capacity of his mind to acquire a living and dynamic contact with truth. What is needed is a renewed confidence in man's ability to regain for himself and others a vision of the world in the light of his own true nature and in the light of his own final goals.

Reconstruction in Philosophy: Aristotle and Dewey

Up to now I have hinted of the need for a reconstruction in philosophy. The reconstruction I have in mind is neither a revived Aristotelianism, nor an expanded naturalism, nor a *carte blanche* acceptance of existentialism as we know it today. The problem with Aristotelianism as we have known it in the past is its too highly traditionalized approach to reality. Aristotelianism as a natural realism is something I readily accept, but it is necessary to get beyond the categories of Aristotle if one is vitally concerned with the problems of contemporary life.

I do not mean, of course, to suggest that Aristotle or any of the ancients is "useless" in our attempt to solve contemporary problems, as there is much, especially in Aristotle's ethics and politics, that is of relevance for our times. However, the time is long past to advocate a simplistic "return to the Greeks" as though Plato, Aristotle, or anyone else had provided a ready-made solution to the problems of life as we know them today. The need therefore is to go *through* and *beyond* both Plato and Aristotle to examine philosophy in a new light.

In more recent times many persons have found this "new light" in Dewey's attempt to construct a philosophy of experience. As I had elsewhere remarked, Dewey had given fresh impetus to that movement initiated in the 19th century, which sought to integrate philosophy and life, even though Dewey's own life and work has covered the first half of the 20th century. Let it be said, therefore, that insofar as Dewey's philosophy is a noteworthy attempt to get philosophy out of its mothball stage, I heartily concur with its basic spirit and aims. What I object to, however, in Dewey is the method by which he tried to accomplish his task—namely, the attempt to base philosophy itself on the methods of the empirical sciences.[3]

Difficult, then, as it is to give an overall evaluation of Dewey's approach to philosophy, this much can and should be said: What is objectionable in Dewey is not his attempt to seek for a reconstruction in philosophy, but his failure to understand *along which lines* such a reconstruction should have taken place. Dewey was eminently right in supposing that philosophy had to be extricated from the epistemological knots in which it had become entangled over the last few hundred years. Yet he was eminently wrong in imagining that the salvation of philosophy was to be had by tailoring the methods of philosophy to the methods of the sciences. As we noted in our previous chapter, there is no intrinsic reason to suppose that philosophers should pre-commit themselves to *any* type of method, scientific or otherwise,

---

3. See Chapter 10, "The Supremacy of Method," in **The Quest for Certainty.** This book was originally presented as the **Gifford Lectures** in 1929 and has more recently been reprinted in paperback form as a Capricorn Books Edition (New York: G. P. Putnam's Sons, 1960).

provided they are faithful to their own ends and goals.

Yet beyond the question of method, there is this further objection to Dewey's philosophy—which lies in his philosophy of man. To him the nature of man (if we can speak of "nature" at all in a philosophy dominated by flux) is the result of the blind evolutionary forces of Nature. The very "life style," if you will, of Dewey's philosophical thought ruled out in advance any attempt to show that in some way man was quite capable—through his intelligence and freedom—of transcending the biological domain. In Dewey's philosophy man is the immanent product of nature, and the measure of human transcendence (if we may use the word at all) lies in our ability to exercise control over nature, nothing more. The important point here is that the biologism of Dewey precluded any attempt to give a satisfactory account, along the lines of a "radical" empiricism, of those deeper wellsprings in the soul of man that enable him to transcend, not only nature, but himself. For Dewey, intelligence itself is a *method*, a device, for resolving the conflicts within the environment, a practical instrument (to use Peirce's expression) "for making ideas clear."

Whether the ideal of clarity, in terms of scientific method, is one that can satisfy the deeper needs of the spirit is a question for the reader to judge, but the point of these remarks is to show that pragmatism, as Dewey interprets it, is hardly in a position to plumb the depths of those needs. But let us proceed at this point—beyond Dewey—to a style of philosophic thought that has enjoyed an immense popularity in yet more recent times, namely, that movement which goes by the name of "existentialism."

What Price Existence?

In the last chapter I spoke of the need for maintaining

26

an "existential" viewpoint in philosophy, and it is my personal conviction that this is the only "point of view" that counts. We must now ask, however, "What is the central contribution of recent existentialist thinkers?" This question no doubt admits of a variety of responses, but my personal response would be this: It is their essential openness to the questions that matter most in philosophy which characterizes the thinking of men like Kierkegaard, Heidegger, Jaspers, Sartre, and Marcel. None of these men are "pure academicians" in the pejorative sense of the term, and all of them, as far as I can tell, have sought some kind of tie-up between philosophy and life. To the great credit of such men philosophy is too free-flowing a *human* activity to become hide-bound by any single type of method or to be poured out into any pre-conceived categories or moulds.

No need here to raise a lengthy discussion as to the "meaning" of existentialism as a philosophy. In the long run existentialism means what each of its advocates claims it to be, which is the equivalent of saying that every man is an existentialist for himself. My own point of interest, however, is to show that however the existentialists may differ among themselves, they all share in common the trait of not leaving you indifferent to their own "point of view." You do not, in other words, read the existentialists as though in a spirit of scientific detachment and remain unscathed as the result of what you have read. What you will find rather in reading them (whether they be atheists, Christians, agnostics), is their aggressive concern with philosophy insofar as it is related to the problems of life.

Yet more specifically than this, existentialism (if we can speak of it as an "ism" at all) is a "crisis" type of philosophy, and to understand what this means, we must get back to the original meaning of the term. To the Greeks "crisis" means

"judgment" in the sense, not merely of an intellectual decision, but in the sense of a living option, "a parting of the
ways." To undergo a crisis means that the needle—however
long it wavers between two extremes—will sooner or later
fall in one direction rather than another, and much the same
holds true of life: no man can ultimately serve two masters,
and the time will come for making a choice between the
two. In this sense, then, existentialism is a philosophy of
crisis insofar as it rids us of the "disease of intellectuals"
who in the absence of any absolute or incontrovertible evidence can never quite make up their mind. As a philosophy
of life, existentialism is an invitation, not just for thinking,
but for acting, for commitment, for engagement in a project
of our choice.

Given such a voluntaristic approach to philosophy it is
no small cause for wonder that existentialists have little
regard for philosophy as an abstract sort of thing that involves the pursuit of concepts, ideas, or reasonings for their
own sake. In fact, much of what we find in their writing is
in the nature of a polemic against "abstraction" as a method
"for making ideas clear." Accordingly, whether we can make
ideas clear or not is not a cause of primary concern. What
does matter is that we learn how to use a psychological
method whereby to unleash the dynamism that lies within
the spirit of man, and this by means of "judgment" in the
apocalyptic sense of the term. Take F. W. Nietzsche (1844-
1900) as a prime example. In his *Thus Spake Zarathustra*
Nietzsche makes no pretense at spinning out concepts, ideas,
demonstrations, or proofs. The entire work rather is in the
nature of an awakening process, a prophecy of things to
come, a call to arms, a kerygma. This, I say, is the general
orientation of existentialists, and however critical we might
be of their methods we should at least grant that these in-

tellectual dynamos, more so than any other group of men, have jolted philosophers (and the world at large) from their dogmatic slumbers.

Wholesome as it may be to maintain such an emphasis as this, the one major weakness of existentialism is this: How long can human nature sustain the type of crisis that the existentialists have been provoking for the last twenty years and more? Sooner or later, it would seem, man finds it necessary to return to some kind of normalcy, and ultimately also, to a condition of sanity and health. Grant, then, that the existentialists have done more than their share to diagnose the problems of life, the question remains: *What have they done to effect anything that resembles a cure?* One need not, of course, look for panaceas, but it is hardly a satisfactory approach to life problems to be assured, as Sartre assures us, that man is "condemned" to freedom. Only if we accept the pessimism that goes with this type of philosophical thinking should we regard ourselves as being in any sense "condemned" at all. Freedom, as I see it, is a gift, a gift of man's nature, and also a challenge to use it to positive ends. If, therefore, the projects in which man engages himself turn out to be no more than useless methods of escape, even as Schopenhauer maintained in the middle of the nineteenth century, why should it be necessary to engage in them at all?

No need here to go into any measure of detail but the basic point of my criticism is this: the problem with the existentialists is generally that of their failure to understand how man in any significant way can orientate himself toward meaningful ends or goals. Having provoked modern man to the point of a crisis in the soul, the existentialists have failed to provide anything of the means whereby that crisis might be resolved. In the meantime modern man exists, so to speak, in a state of suspended animation—like Avi-

29

cenna's floating man—without any direction or goal. One is reminded too of a surgeon who knows how to open up a patient's wound but is completely inept at being able to provide the necessary stitches for its repair. Sometimes too the surgery is so radical that one wonders whether there is anything left of the patient at all.

Concluding Remark

In the present chapter I have tried in some way to show the need for a new direction in philosophy. The method of the analytic linguists, for all of its positive value as a propedeutic to philosophic inquiry, is altogether too narrow to provide for the deeply-rooted needs of the human spirit, its craving for freedom, its overall meaning and purpose, and finally, for the dynamism of life itself. A resort to pure Aristotelianism is too tradition-bound an approach to solve contemporary problems, to say nothing of the fact that the method of the Greeks was itself heavily tainted with a kind of rationalism of its own. As for the development of contemporary philosophy in America, Dewey made a thoroughgoing attempt to effect a reconstruction in philosophy, but entirely along the lines of an earth-bound naturalism that makes little or no provision for the needs of the human spirit. Finally, the existentialists have pointed up radically what these needs are, but have failed to discern the means whereby they might be fulfilled. What remains for us now is to develop an approach to philosophy that will enable it to take a new turn—in the direction of unifying and integrating those elements of human experience that have been disjointed and separated for hundreds of years. As I hope to explain in the second part of this volume this new direction in philosophy may best be called that of an "integral realism."

3

THE
TYRANNY
OF FALSE
IDEAS

Introduction

THAT MODERN
man has suffered a peculiar state of unrest is abundantly
clear to anyone who has been through the last few decades.
Pragmatism, linguistic analysis, scepticism, existentialism,
the revival of thomism, Ayn Rand "objectivism," the God-is-
Dead movement, or what have you, are all indications of
the diversity of thought that is characteristic of our times.
Pluralism, a healthy-minded pluralism, is a sign of progress
and growth. Yet confusion of thought, especially in the modern varieties of scepticism, is a sign of disintegration and decay. As a friend of mine once remarked, there is no greater
softness than the softness of the head.

A Restatement of the Problem

In the past two chapters I have spoken of the need for a
philosophy with a sense of direction. The time has come in
all areas of inquiry to get beyond the maze of words into
a realm of knowledge that will enable men to rediscover
some sense of purpose in their lives. As it was once said by
St. Thomas (1225-1274) in the Introduction to his book,
De Ente Et Essentia, a small error in the beginning

31

can lead, in the end, to total confusion. What, then, *is* the error that has diverted the modern mind in its quest for wisdom and truth? More than anything else, I would say, it is the presupposition (initiated by Descartes and developed by Berkeley and Hume) that the mind knows nothing else than its own ideas. In a later chapter I shall explore at some length the foundations of classical modern subjectivism, but the point I wish to make now is that the *natural realism* of the human intelligence has been stopped up as it were, like a stream from its course, into channels that are filled with all sorts of myths and illusions.

While the truth therefore in its unabashed simplicity is always easy to see for him who is disposed to see it, such is not generally the case with modern man. Modern man in spite of his best intentions has been so heavily bombarded with subjectivism on all sides as not to have emerged unscathed from the battle of conflicting ideas. His situation is in no way different from Plato's men in the cave whose eyes have become so accustomed to the shadows and appearances of reality that should anyone point out to them the "really real" they would deny its very existence.

It is in this precise setting, then, that I see the need for a reconstruction in philosophy. The need, as I see it, is not for a greater multiplicity of superficial ideas, but for an attempt to achieve on a fundamental level a far greater simplicity than has marked any philosophy in the past few hundred years. Lest the significance of this point be lost, consider that whenever philosophy is in a state of decline it is marked by a failure to achieve a unifying, integrating principle that will serve to give us some insight, however inadequate, into the ultimate nature of life. Thus was it in the time of the stoics and sceptics, and so it is today; the intelligence of modern man is so overladen with the complications of older systems of thought as to have rendered itself incapable of seeing the truth for itself in a new and fresh light.[1]

Given this to be so, the task for the philosopher today is to carve out a new path—in the direction, not of a useless syncretism of the systems of the past, but in the direction of the development of a new approach to philosophy that will mark a return to the idea of wisdom as therapy, as "understanding of life." Unfortunately the modern mind is itself in no small measure the result of what philosophers themselves have made it out to be over the last few hundred years. It is, if you will, an amalgam of all sorts of conflicting ideas and opinions that have led, not to the enlightenment of the individual, as it had been hoped for since the eighteenth century and beyond, but to a radical incapacity on his part to think for himself. The great need of our times, therefore is that of "re-doing" the modern mind, not by the substitution of one kind of brainwashing for another, but by an attempt to nurse it back to a condition of health. The problem is to re-introduce the mind to its natural inheritance of those simple truths which, provided the obstacles are removed, it can and should see for itself. This task can be accomplished moreover without any kind of brainwashing or propaganda and, for that matter, without any specialized method of scientific technique and control.

Ideas and Their Influence on Our Lives

Most persons have little or no conception of the all-per-

---

1. It is one thing to be aware of the importance of past ideas, but quite another to do nothing more with them than to reshape them into eclectic systems of our own. Eclecticism in philosophy means simply the borrowing of a wide variety of ideas from different systems of thought without any proportionate attempt to see them in a new and unified light.

vasive influence of ideas on their personal lives. Imagining themselves to be immune, as it were, from the influence of other men's minds, they flatter themselves into thinking that they are the sole progenitors of their own methods and ideas. No assumption or hypothesis, however, could be farther removed from the truth. As I see it, the truth of the matter is quite simply this: every age, society, and culture is characterized by what the Germans call a "Zeitgeist"—a "spirit of the times"—a spirit which is marked by the predominance of certain ideas and values over others of a previous age which no longer hold sway.

As an example in question, no rationalist of the seventeenth or eighteenth century could possibly have dreamed of the extent to which the later Freudian idea of the unconscious would someday dominate much of Western society as we know it today.[2] In the eighteenth century it had been *assumed*—and this was one of the leading ideas *of that particular time*—that Reason itself (with a capital "R") could be established as a method of control over all human conduct, individual and social alike. The only problem for the rationalists, as it was for Descartes earlier, was that of finding out the right *method* of control.

Today almost no one assumes that society could ever be maneuvered into a position of complete rational control,

---

2. Incidentally, and by a strange twist of paradox the modern notion of the "unconscious" and "subconscious" was anticipated in the rationalistic psychology of G. W. Leibniz (1646-1716) who takes into account the reality of what he calls "minute perceptions" prior, that is, to their appearance on the level of conscious perception. Yet in spite of this little known fact, my statement still holds: no rationalist, including Leibniz, could possibly have dreamed of the influence of this later development on society as we know it today.

The Tyranny of False Ideas

given the notion of the unconscious dynamism of *all* human behavior. On the level of popular culture, this means that modern man has been so profoundly shaken in his previous conviction as to the supremacy of human reason and its control over human life that he has all but capitulated to the influence of a psychological determinism which in its own way is just as rigid and uncompromising as any of the earlier forms of Calvinism.

Although philosophy therefore bakes no bread, it is the sort of thing—given the profound influence of ideas on people's lives—that men live by just as really as they do by the bread they eat. If we may paraphrase scripture on this point: It is not by bread alone that men live but—for good or for ill—by the impact that ideas have on their lives. It is not therefore a question *whether* ideas influence our behavior or not, but only *which ones* and *to what extent.* No doubt it was for reasons of this sort that John Locke (1632-1704) took his famous inventory of ideas in his long-standing classic, *An Essay On Human Understanding.* As best I can make out, Locke was convinced of the need to test our ideas by experience rather than to accept them uncritically —that is, as assumptions that have no foundation in fact.[3]

Not to be misled from our central point, let us then note that ideas are as much a reality in our lives as television,

3. I do not, of course, speak approvingly of Locke except for the motivations that underlay his work. Actually, his own method of classifying ideas was a faulty one, since it was based on the Cartesian pre-supposition that the direct object of mind can only be its own ideas. While Locke therefore rejected the innatism of Descartes, he unwittingly was influenced by the implicit subjectivism of the Cartesian technique. By way of contrast, the form of realism I propose in the latter half of this book has little in common with the inferential realism of Descartes, Locke, or any one of the other classical modern forms.

planes, radar, or whatever else you choose to name. Make a biological comparison, if you will, between ideas and germs, and you will find (in the making of this comparison) that many persons are the "germ-carriers of ideas" without ever realizing themselves the extent to which their own ideas (if indeed the ideas in question *are* their own) exert an influence on other men's lives. And if this be true, is it not futile to imagine that men can inoculate themselves from the ideas—hidden or otherwise—of the culture and society in which they live? Surprisingly enough to some, the difference between an educated man and one who is not, is not the failure to be influenced by ideas, but rather the element of choice involved. The uncultured, uncritical person is unwittingly, unconsciously manipulated *by* ideas, in popular magazines and all the other channels of communication. He is, so to speak, the unconscious victim of ideas whether the idea in question be as pervasive in its consequences as that of a psychological determinism which totally denies human freedom or as *apparently* trivial and innocuous as the latest attempt to show the arbitrariness of all sexual morality.

Ideas, then, whether they are consciously held or not have an influence on people's lives, and given all this to be so, society has a right to expect of its philosophers some kind of intellectual leadership. This means, first of all, that the philosophers—above any other class of men in society—should be on the lookout for false ideas with a view toward protecting the public against them, not by a method of suppression, but by a method of analysis and exposé. Yet from a more positive and constructive point of view it is also incumbent upon philosophers to enable society to achieve a better understanding of itself through the development of new and creative ideas that are in harmony with

36

human nature. On this last point one should never overlook the fact that ideas, apart from their speculative worth, can and do serve as plans of action, and unless there is some kind of vision, it is literally true that the people will perish. To the extent therefore that philosophers can help the public to see old truths in a fresh light and to acquire a new level of vision, they can and will play a more effective role in society than if they were to confine themselves to a narrow specialty of their own. In contrast, then, to such an enlarged view as this, it should never be said of the philosopher that he himself is the unconscious victim of ideas that are patently false.[4]

Symptoms or Causes?

It has long been my conviction as a philosopher that few things are as harmful in one's life as a false idea. Normally, people act according to what they know or think they know, and in my judgment much "abnormal" behavior is the direct and immediate result of a conscious or semi-conscious indulgence in a false idea. I am hardly proposing, of course, that knowledge by itself will cure people's lives. Yet in spite of this fact it is quite true to say that modern life is plagued with all sorts of myths like the myth of the total dominance in man of unconscious motives of behavior. However the myths themselves would be harmless were it not for the fact that modern man has given them a credence that he has given to few religious dogmas and it is his belief in them

4. Part of what I am saying is that there are fads in the realm of ideas even as there are fads in the area of dress, and it is especially important for philosophers not to be "taken in" by these fads, but to the contrary to warn the public against them whenever the occasion demands.

(the myths, not the dogmas) that has led to every kind of neurotic disorder. The problem then in achieving any kind of cure is to get beyond the myths and the half-truths to an understanding in depth of the ultimate reality of human nature.

Unfortunately, however, modern psychology has not been as helpful in this regard as it often claims to be, especially in view of the fact that some of the myths of Freudianism have become a self-fulfilling prophecy.[5] This is to say that there is much in the use of psychology—to the extent that some of it is based on myths—that has led to more harm than good. Yet apart from the matter of the questionable use of psychology, there is this further item to consider: as I see it, the problem with modern man is not merely to help him, as indeed psychologists do, to lead a "normal" life. The problem rather is to help him to fulfill his basic needs, including the needs of the spirit. On this point I make bold to say that few practicing psychiatrists are sufficiently aware, in my judgment, of the underlying *causes* of the conflicts that emerge in the lives of their patients. It is enough for them rather to "cure" their patients of the symptoms of this neurotic order or that in the hope that the patient may resume his regular domestic and working routine.

I have no objection, of course, to the practice of psychiatry in this limited sense of the term. But I should want to make it perfectly clear that any presupposition that would

---

5. I include in the list of Freudian myths the reduction of religion in psychologistic terms to the idea of God as "father image," the dogma of pan-sexualism, and the **exaggerated** use of symbolism in the psychoanalytic technique. In making these criticisms, however, I do not excoriate, as the behaviorists do, psychoanalytic technique as a method for effecting cures. My only point is that the use of the technique should be dissociated from some of the original myths from which it took its rise.

regard man—in purely behavioristic terms as an animal and nothing significantly more—is not only bad philosophy, but bad psychology as well. In other words, it is a mistaken vision, on the part of psychiatrists, to see the needs of their patients in an exclusively biological light. No doubt there are the day-to-day problems in psychiatry of helping to cure their patients of everything from bed wetting to the excessive use of alcoholic drink. However, neither the cure of the symptoms of these habits nor the cure of the habits themselves is a sufficient means of the cure of their underlying causes.

The need therefore on the part of the psychiatrist is that of realizing the limitations of his own specific methods of cure. Nor would it be reasonable on the part of the philosopher, or, for that matter, of a theologian, to expect the psychiatrist as such to have any strong positive insights into the intellectual and spiritual disorders that underlie the more superficial conflicts of modern life. Under normal circumstances (if ever they are normal) it is enough for the psychiatrist to know that these disorders (such as the total absence of guilt in a patient who *should* feel guilty) do exist—to know that they are real.[6]

If this is the case, then it is a matter of great importance that we make a proper assessment of the work of the philosopher in relation to the needs of his fellowman. Is the philosopher merely one specialist among others who is serving,

---

6. I am insistent on this point in view of the almost universally prevalent assumption among psychologists, behaviorist psychologists in particular, as to the identity of symptoms and causes. What is important therefore is that more and more psychologists begin to recognize the radically spiritual dimension of the problems of many of their patients—without any attempt on their part to **reduce** these problems to matters of simple adjustment and control.

THE BETRAYAL OF WISDOM

on a purely horizontal level, to advance the frontiers of knowledge, and nothing more? If my first two chapters are correct, the search for a true philosophy goes far beyond that of a purely empirical approach to the problem of knowledge as such. It extends rather into the realm of the spirit, since one of the fundamental goals of philosophy is the discovery of that kind of knowledge which I call "intellectus vitae"—an *understanding of life*. However, it is not enough merely to *understand* life to be a good philosopher: one must also learn how to *direct* life into channels that are ultimately meaningful and significant if the role of the philosopher as wise man is to be "played." In the latter part of the twentieth century, even as in earlier times, it belongs to the wise man to place things in order and *there is nothing more important than the order to be placed in people's lives.* All in all, then, my point simply is this: the work of the philosopher is to treat, not merely symptoms, but causes. It is a work that requires him to effect a cure in the root, not merely in the branches, and the kind of cure that will lead the intellect of modern man to the rediscovery of those truths, easily discoverable, but also easily lost sight of, which have been obscured by the impact of subjectivism.

Translated into practical terms, the point just made raises the issue as to whether it is possible for man to use his intelligence in every area of secondary concern, in the area of what St. Augustine calls "inferior reason," and yet fall short in the knowledge of his fundamental goals in life. Such a thing no doubt is *possible* since many persons *are* confused as to their fundamental goals. But the point I wish to make is this: Should modern man *resign* himself to a situation as radically inconsistent as this or should he not rather do the best in his power to remedy it—by taking stock of the powers that do lie at his disposal for re-directing the course of his life?

Rhetorical as the question may sound, it is one that pertains to the root issue of the "proper object" of the intelligence of man. Shall we suppose, as the pragmatists do, that the only "proper object" of intelligence is its immediate practical use? Or should we not say to the contrary that the "use" of intelligence is most appropriately served whenever it is directed *in depth* to an understanding of the meaning of life itself?

In answer to such questions as these we must here keep in mind that nothing is so self-defeating as that very attitude and frame of mind whereby it is assumed at the outset that the task at hand lies beyond one's natural capacities when in point of fact it lies within everyone's reach. I am no advocate, of course, of the type of "philosophy" which attempts to heal men's minds by the method of "self-cure" whereby one keeps repeating that he is "getting better and better" by the day. But the question here is not one of self-hypnosis. It is a question rather of the need for regaining a sense of confidence in certain powers and capacities within the very nature of man that have been atrophied for the past few hundred years.

But let me return to my point. Defeatism, of whatever sort, says that the "job" is impossible before any effective measures are taken to see whether it is possible or not. It is an attitude which prescribes inaction on the ground that, *whichever* alternative is followed, the result will be the same as if no course of action had been taken at all. This, as I see, is the disease of "inactionists." In their failure to realize that the "will to believe" is an integral part of life, the "inactionists" fail to know also that the intelligence of man is naturally endowed to know something about the truth of life itself.

Although I am therefore persuaded that an attitude of faith, confidence, or the "will-to-believe" is essential to life's fulfillment, I reject that part of pragmatism which denies that there is such a thing as truth in a purely objective sense. In other words, it is a pure fiction to suppose—in respect to the basic truths of life—that man is in a position of having to invent his own truths. Far from this being so, the human intelligence is teleologically oriented to the knowledge of truth even as the wings of a bird are made to fly. But what *kind* of truth, you might add? Certainly the salvation of mankind does not lie in multiplying truths of fact, and in any case it is quite possible to discover such truths through the use of computerized machines. Truth, as I speak of it here, is something far more than knowledge of facts, figures, or rules since it implies nothing less than a genuine insight into what we might unabashedly speak of as the truth and the mystery of *being*.

Simplistic as the expression may sound, it is incumbent on man to rediscover for himself, not in a purely logical fashion, but in very concrete terms, the meaning of "what is" in such terms as it is meaningful for life. The mind of man is not, as it were, like a vacuum which can operate in abstraction from the real or "existential" world; rather, it is a dynamic function which relates and inter-relates to an objective order of events in men's lives. Hence, contrary to the attitude of sceptics, the problem for man is not *whether* he can know reality—but rather what are the *means* by which such knowledge can be attained?

As a start in the right direction I would suggest the need for a fundamental openness to reality of the sort by which man opens up his mind to the truth by methods other than

that of the "method of frontal attack." One cannot, as it
were, demand on the spot to have or acquire a comprehen-
sive knowledge of the "mystery of being" but should, as it
were, allow himself to *grow* and *develop* in the truth—on
a step by step basis and as the nature of his personal limits
or situation requires or demands. In other words, no one
can learn the truth (of whatever kind) all at once, but only
by degrees and according to one's capacity to learn, and
here we should be mindful of the wisdom of an old scholastic
axiom or maxim which suggests that anything an individual
or person "receives" is according to the limits or nature of
the "receiver" "Quidquid recipitur secundum modum re-
cipientis recipitur"). On a very practical level this means
that you can either overwhelm an individual by giving him
too much all at once (with all the unhappy moral or psychological consequences that are attendant upon such an
approach as by an overdose of sex education in a child who
is not prepared to receive it) or you can starve an individual
by giving him nothing at all as when you abstain from giving
him a religious education until he is twenty one years old.

The soul of man, and I use this word without apologies,
needs above all to be nursed back to health, and by "health"
in this sense I mean a condition of being that results from
the wholesome interplay in realistic terms between man and
his external environment. I am not, of course, a Deweyan
environmentalist, least of all of the behaviorist variety. But
what I am stressing here is man's fundamental need for a
redeeming contact, first on the level of the senses, and then
on the level of his whole being—intelligence, emotions, and
will—with *being*, and all that it implies in basic metaphysical
terms, as it is given him in the world outside of himself. Man
is not a solitary creature who can for long isolate himself

from his environment in the hopes of regaining his lost consciousness of the ultimately real.

The "ultimately real," however we may try to describe it in non-absolutistic terms—is too elusive and dynamic a thing to be captured by any *a priori* categories of our own mind. And the problem here, which is that of establishing a primordial contact with the real *as given,* is not a problem of closed categories, but of an openness to *being* of the sort by which we adapt ourselves and our intelligence to the given rather than the other way around. This means that the intelligence of man should be open to the "given" in *whatever* form it is given to him, whether by way of revelation, that is to say, of a divinely revealed truth which transcends the powers of reason, or whether by way of the natural truths of reason itself. In fact, these are the only two ways by which it is possible for man to *grow* in the truth—either or both of which have been rejected by modern man in his desperate, voluntaristic attempt to achieve a mythical "freedom," which is also a suicidal one, of his native intelligence.

The Courage to Act and the Dynamism of Human Life

This much for now concerning the right use of intelligence. In our chapter on the "Centrality of Prudence" we shall say more. Yet before we conclude this Chapter some few notes are necessary to speak of the need for making what Tillich has called "the leap of faith." But a moment ago I endeavored to show that no idea is more "false" than the one which prohibits us from acting at the moment when action is ripe. To believe, in other words, in the inevitability of failure at the very moment when—through action—success is knocking at our door—is to indulge oneself in a colossal delusion.

44

The Tyranny of False Ideas

Yet the tendency not to act when the moment for action is ripe is all too prevalent a thing in human nature to allow us to dismiss it out of hand. Human nature by inclination plays the role of the conservative in its persistent refusal to make the necessary "leap of faith." The quest for certainty —of the *wrong* kind—impels us to cling to the present order of things, as though that order could against overwhelming odds be preserved against every reasonable attempt to change it.

. The truth of the matter is, however, that in spite of the essential continuity of life the essence of life itself is that of a growth process that cannot be effectively withheld or repressed. Whether you speak of it as the "pre-conscious" or the "unconscious" or the "subconscious," or even as the "superconscious," there is, as Henri Bergson (1859-1941) correctly notes, an essential element of dynamism in all life processes as such which tends to resist all tendencies to the contrary. In this sense Darwinism as a philosophy is profoundly true, insofar as there is a kind of survival of the fittest—though I should hesitate to interpret this principle in purely biological terms. Those who identify themselves, through whatever risk is involved, with the development of the processes of life are those who, so to speak, utilize their energies in "riding the waves." On the other hand, those who resist (let us call them "resistors") are predestined to become professional losers if only for the reason that they consume their own vital energies in opposing those goals that are immanent to human life itself. In this very process of misguided opposition the "resistors" are those who play the game all too conservatively and in so doing consume the whole of their energies in a direction opposed (futilely so) to the fulfillment of life, and so in a suicidal act pave the way to their own ultimate frustration.

45

Here, then, we encounter in a modern scientific setting, and on the level of modern psychology, the profound truth of the gospel—"nisi granum frumenti cadit in terram, ipsum solum manet." (Unless the grain of seed falls into the ground, it remaineth alone). Life is such, in other words, that its inherent dynamism is ultimately irrepressible. Any attempts to repress it for a time are only a partial, an apparent success, a holding action, but no less than an ultimate failure. Even as it had been spoken to Paul of Tarsus—"It is not good for you to kick against the goad," so too every psychological attempt to "kick against the goad" results always and ultimately—if the "kicking" is persistent and pertinacious—in the disruption of the human personality.

One therefore either obeys the laws of human nature (taken in relation to its discoverable ends) or engages himself in a senseless battle to thwart the ultimate designs of human life taken in relation to God, nature, and fellow man, and the choice (although made over a long period of time, let us say, over fifty or eighty years) is in the end irrevocable. As for the use of time in the present, man was not made by his Creator to stand still, but to move forward, and the meaning of time is to seize the opportunity of "moving forward," of "redeeming the time," even when at a given moment one is *seemingly* standing still. Wherein, then, does this forward movement of the "soul," indeed of the whole man, consist? In choosing, I would suppose, a path of wisdom that is constantly on the lookout for signs or symbols of one's vocation, of what a future course of action should be. But not only this. At a certain point—when all the discernible evidence is "in" one should then be prepared to act without further delay. *The right action at the right time is equally as much a part of wisdom as all the deliberation that preceded it,* and if we keep this point in mind we shall discover that

46

The Tyranny of False Ideas

Falstaff was profoundly wrong *in context* when he said that "discretion is the better part of valor." If "discretion" here means "precipitant action," he is right, of course, but the axiom obscures the positive truth that *action* (rightly informed) is the *better* part of valor and without it there is neither prudence *nor* valor.

If we may borrow a note from Paul Tillich (1886-1965), it is incumbent upon all to have the courage to be. Such courage, however, is meaningless unless it means the courage to *become* what we are not at any given moment. What matters therefore is that the sons of Adam and Eve develop the courage to grow—not in *any* direction like so many weeds in a garden—but in the direction that is suited to their own unique vocation in life and in a manner proportioned to their talents and circumstances whatever they may be.

Conclusion

Above all else it is the task of the philosopher as therapist to liberate the human intelligence from the shackles of ignorance, whether in the area of education, art, morality, or religion. Philosophy properly understood can, and should, play a liberating role—thus making it possible for modern man to regain the lost vision of himself and of the world in which he lives. Kierkegaard was deeply right when he spoke of a "sickness unto death": modern man is sick unto death with a sickness of soul that has atrophied his powers with respect to their proper objects. Yet the greatest tragedy of all is the atrophy of the human intelligence, and the problem here is not that man has used his reason and ended up with the wrong conclusion. The problem rather is his complete failure to use his reason at all, a failure which has led to paralysis. To overcome this paralysis modern man must purge his subconscious of all the false ideas that have pervaded modern culture and prepare himself, in a modern sense, for a re-adaptation to the needs of his soul. But this is what the next chapter is about.

4

IMPOSSIBLE
DREAMS
AND THE
MODE OF
THEIR
DELIVER-
ANCE

*Introductory
Remarks*

THE PRESENT
stalemate of philosophy, especially in the United States, has
deprived modern man of one of the greatest means of knowing how to resolve the conflicts that confront him in contemporary life. The image of a philosopher as a man in an
ivory tower is altogether too true with reference to most
philosophers as we know them today. Better yet, it might be
truer to say that the public at large has no image of the
philosopher at all.

What, then, *are* the benefits of philosophy as they relate
to the ordinary man? Or is it asking too much for everyone to become a philosopher? Questions of this sort are not
easy to answer, but I would venture to say that everyone—
whether he intends to become a *professional* philosopher or
not—should become a philosopher for himself. This seem-

ingly cryptic statement has no hidden meaning except to show that philosophy of whatever sort should be a personal reflection on experience, especially of the kind of experience that takes place in the depths of the soul. As for the benefits of this type of knowing, we can say only this—that philosophy, in its deepest sense, can enable man to recapture the full dimension of himself. So conceived and developed philosophy can and should become for modern man, not a method of escape from reality, but a method of coming to grips with the ultimate questions of life. It is in this sense that I shall speak in this chapter of "catering to the needs of the soul."

Self-Knowledge

The problem with modern man is that he has become a stranger to himself. Everyone knows, of course, that two people who refuse to communicate with each other often begin fabricating myths about each other's character and much the same holds true about the ignorance we have of ourselves. Not knowing who we are interiorly we begin at first to "make believe" (as many philosophers have) that the interior self in the Augustinian sense does not exist, and in punishment for this denial the interior self begins to take its revenge. As a result a deep sense of restlessness ensues, and the "external man" begins to invent all sorts of mechanisms whereby to distract himself from the reality that lies beneath. This distraction may take the form of an unwonted competition in business, an aggressive pursuit of a "happy" family life, or an unflagging devotion to "duty." Yet the greater the number of distractions, the deeper the conflicts that arise.

But let us get back to the question of self-knowledge. Is

it not true that man, modern man, has forgotten the wisdom of Socrates' maxim "Know thyself"? "Know thyself," not only in terms of the job you hold, or the restaurants you patronize, or the size of the mortgage on your house—but "know thyself" by a penetrating interior knowledge that searches to the depths of your soul. As for the means of such knowledge, suffice it to say that it cannot be had by a kind of neurotic "crash program," but only by an openness of mind whereby one learns to read between the lines of the events in one's life. It is the result of what I have already referred to as *intellectus vitae*—an understanding, in contrast to mere knowledge, of life. We come to know ourselves in and through a certain manner of silence that is deeply rooted in the inner recesses of the soul.

Self-Love

Self-knowledge, of course, is one thing and self-love, another. Paradoxically, few persons love themselves in the sense of getting beyond their own selfish concerns such as the concern for a full stomach and a ready bottle of wine. Self-love, as I speak of it here, is an active cultivation of the needs of the soul, and it implies a tactical retreat from others as to discover for ourselves who we are as persons, and not as functional objects of someone else's whims or fancies. For those who are activists it means a willingness to change one's life in the direction, not of more action, but of a certain type of passivity whereby one allows the *truth of things* to sink into the depths of one's being. Self-love means the abandonment for a time of all exterior activity to cultivate a sense of freedom and peace whereby we come to be "at one" with ourselves, and at this point a ready example comes to mind. During the later sixties, at the height of the peace

3

demonstrations which demanded an end of American military involvement in Vietnam, some few youngsters placed a very significant sign on their backs which read, "Peace begins with me." The obvious point of the maxim was that there can be no world peace unless it first begins to reside in the breasts of individual men and women, and to this we might add that peace is always, as St. Augustine once pointed out, the tranquillity of order. Where there is no order neither is it possible to have any kind of peace.

Old-fashioned, then, as the remedy may seem, modern man must return to the Pythagorean notion of philosophy as a way of life, and by this I do not mean such external practices as abstention from beans. The secret rather of the Pythagorean way of life lay in their notion of "catering" or "tending" to the needs of the soul. Thus to the Pythagoreans there were three types of men like the people at the Olympic games: athletes, merchants, and spectators. The athletes were men of action so busy with the winning of the race that they had no time for anything else. The merchants were those who came neither to play the game nor to watch it, but only to make money. Only the spectators sought the game as a matter of pure enjoyment and for its own sake. If, therefore, we compare life itself to the games, we find that the person who enjoys it most is not the activist (the athlete), nor the merchant, but the spectator for whom life itself has a deeper meaning of its own that escapes the ordinary participant.

Modern Man and the Cult of Illusion

In spite of his frantic efforts to make money, to gain fame, to find fulfillment in sex, modern man neither knows nor loves himself. He has utterly failed in the language of the Pythagoreans to "cater to the needs of the soul." To add to the disappointment and confusion, philosophers themselves have dismissed any talk of the "soul" as a "bit of medieval lore" as though having nothing to do with their own particular field of specialization. What they overlook, of course, is the fact that truth, even on a purely natural plane, has a certain healing power of its own, and conversely, whenever the human intelligence is deprived of its object, then it is not only the "mind" that suffers but indeed *the whole man*. What man lacks today is integrity, not in the narrow moral sense of the term as "honesty," but in the broader ontological sense of "wholeness," "inner harmony" of being, or of what I myself prefer to call a sense of "integral realism."

Interestingly enough, the Pythagoreans, in spite of the rigid dualism of their psychology, did feel the need, even as did Plato later, of the restoration of a certain "harmony" within the soul. In fact, the whole educational theory of Plato is based on the presupposition that music, mathematics, and philosophy (in an ascending order of importance) were the proper instruments for restoring the imbalance man suffered from his failure to tend to the needs of the soul.

We need not confine our attention, however, to the Greeks since it is modern man that is the primary object of our concern. And the question that continues to plague us is this: "Why is modern man so much of a problem to himself?" At this point I venture to say that for want of self-knowledge and self-love modern man has gotten himself miserably confused about the fundamental goals of life, and in so doing has lost his basic sense of identity which, independently of any of the kind of activities in which he engages, marks off the very kind of being that he is. Not knowing who he is, he fails to pursue those kinds of goods that are appropriate to the fullness of his nature and dignity as a man.

The problem, then, with modern man is not a failure on his part to seek what he himself considers to be good. *Everyone* seeks out the good. The problem, however, lies in the search of those goods that are for him only apparent and not real goods, as though the search for ultimate meaning could be equated in the long run with alcohol, sex, power, knowledge, money, physical health, or fame. I do not mean to suggest, of course, that the above-mentioned goods are only an illusion of sense. Money, for example, is no illusion. In a non-barter society it is one of the basic necessities of life. Yet as an end in itself—as the very goal of all human striving—it does become a fantastic illusion since it not only fails to provide for the basic needs of the spirit, but perverts them to a false end, thus becoming like pride itself the root of all evil.

But let me develop this notion of the cult of illusion. There is an immense reserve, so it seems, in the intelligence of man for creating illusions, and the history of philosophy itself is a witness to the fact. As a prime example consider the doctrine—initiated by Descartes and perpetuated by the empirical tradition—that the mind of man is confined to its own states. This doctrine, maintained by rationalists and empiricists alike, is based on a denial of the fact that the world and the people in it exist even as we perceive them to be. It is the illusion of subjectivism as we know it today: your truth is your truth, and mine is my own, and seldom do the twain ever meet. But where does the remedy lie? Certainly not in working out a more refined epistemology along the lines of subjectivism, but only by getting off on a new track. The need, as I see it, is to effect a reconstruction in philosophy of the sort that will lead man back into integral realism in the areas of psychology, ethics, and politics. But more of this later.

What I want to say now is that if modern man wishes to extricate himself from the cult of illusion, he must make a clean break with the errors of the past. In other words, there is no point in canonizing these errors so as to guarantee their influence for all time to come. It may be true that false ideas (like monsters at birth) are slated to die a natural death, but the truth of the matter is that all too often they die hard. Accordingly, it is evil, not just for the *mind* of man, but for *man himself,* to be deprived of the truth. Take a paranoic for example. The illusion he suffers of being persecuted by everyone he meets would be harmless enough if it lodged only in his head. But the problem lies also in his soul and it expresses itself in his external conduct. Everyone acts, in some sense, according to what he knows or thinks he knows. Yet on the more positive side, the truth once known in a practical way has the power to make man free. This does not mean that there is a simple equation between knowledge and virtue, but only that a true understanding of the deeper dimensions of life's problems *and nothing less than that* will lead to their proper solution. Thus everyone tends to act according to what he knows and the person who knows himself, on the level of the depths of the soul, will get beyond the superficialities of life in a way that an unreflecting person cannot. The true healing of the human intelligence invariably points the way to the healing of the total man, and given the accomplishment of this objective, society itself will suffer no small measure of improvement.

The Worship of Method and Its Baneful Effects

To persuade modern man that he is something more than

a biological unit is one of the greatest challenges to philosophy today. No one, of course, will deny that science and technology have brought immense benefits to mankind. Yet it is simply false to imagine that the physical and social sciences can by themselves resolve what we have called in this book "the problem of modern man."[1] As one writer has said: "The society which creates scientists by diminishing the ranks of its philosophers may in the end have little need for either." The point of this quote is to show that neither the physical nor the social sciences can provide answers to the ultimate problems of life whereas philosophy, as envisioned in its traditional role, can at least show the way. It is not a question therefore of "either" philosophy "or" science, but of "both" existing in integral relationship with each other, and by philosophy here I mean, not the study of method as such, but philosophy as wisdom of life.

For the sake of historical perspective let us take note of the fact that philosophy to this day failed to rescue itself from the epistemological knots in which it became entwined since the days of Hume and Kant. Having paralyzed itself through the super-imposition of categories of its own making, philosophy has rejected those categories that are naturally discoverable in a world of genuinely human experience. The problem with philosophers today is no longer that of a dogmatic slumber, but to the contrary it is that of a sceptical paralysis which makes it all but impossible for the modern mind to get an overall view of the problems, both individual and social, of human life.

1. This is the problem of helping modern man to rediscover himself. It is the problem, if you will, of resolving the "identity crisis" that has resulted from the collapse of many of the older structures that have molded that peculiar being whom we call "Western man."

Impossible Dreams

In the personal view of this author philosophy as well as any other intellectual discipline needs to be kept alive, and the only way to keep it alive, or better to *make* it live for each new generation is to bring philosophy to bear with all of its traditional wisdom and insights on present problems, on present situations, and on present experience. Too many philosophers, in other words, are either too much orientated toward the past as past or, as in Dewey's case, toward the future, and too little concerned with a deep inner reflection on present experience.

Later in this volume I want to say more on the meaning of philosophy as a reflection on man's *total* experience. For now I want to show that philosophers today have by and large suffered a loss of nerve, and in so doing have failed to provide the direction that modern society, especially the youth of our day, most crucially needs. But to understand why this is so we need to renew our sense of historical perspective. Consider, then, the fact that philosophy at one time (and *for too long a time*, indeed), was polymathic in character, embracing as it did, practically *all* knowledge for its domain. In the days of Aristotle and for a long time thereafter, philosophy *was* physics, biology, psychology, sociology, and all the rest. But with the advent of science, roughly since the time of Kepler, Galileo, and Newton, philosophy gradually suffered a loss of prestige in consequence of which some thinkers felt the need of reform.

No doubt there were many reasons why philosophers like Descartes and Bacon felt the need of reform, but the most potent of them all was the growing suspicion that philosophers had been using the wrong *method* all along. The "key" therefore to the "reform of learning" was that of finding some new method that would put philosophy on the same foundation as the physical sciences themselves. No need here to go into the particular methods proposed by different types of philosophers, interesting as such an exploration would be. My point, however, is that the *aim* of every major philosopher during the classical modern period was to provide some kind of method that would do for philosophy what the experimental method was doing for the advancement of science.

Noble as were the intentions of its authors, the initiators of the "modern way" in philosophy became so pre-occupied with the question of method that it became for them and most philosophers since their time a kind of obsessional neurosis. The result of such a pursuit, namely, that of a single method of philosophizing, did in the end lead, even among philosophers themselves, to the radical disillusionment concerning all philosophical knowledge as such. Most especially, since the advent of logical positivism, philosophers have become so self-conscious concerning the problem of method that they have virtually abandoned all attempts in the direction of a true creativity that would put philosophy like science on a new path. While the scientists then, from Galileo to Einstein, had given themselves free rein in projecting bolder and bolder hypotheses in the area of their proper domain, many of the world's philosophers have been in a mood of retrenchment that has cut philosophy off from the very problems that had sustained it for more than 2,000 years. Many philosophers, in short, have abandoned philosophy in order to become the handmaidens of science.[2]

2. The present state of intellectual bankruptcy in the philosophical world is an indication that the creative energies of philosophers have remained latent and undeveloped in favor of a quest for certainty (along scientific lines) that scientists themselves have abandoned. Along these lines I suggest as excellent collateral reading for this and the preceeding

Impossible Dreams

The Need for a Restoration to Health

In the present volume we are confronted with the need for establishing two fundamental theses: (1) that philosophy itself has a fundamental need for being restored to a condition of health, and (2) that the restoration of philosophy, in the sense I intend it, as an integral realism and as a radical empiricism of the human spirit, can well provide for the kind of therapy that our society needs today. As to the need for restoring philosophy itself to a condition of health the predominant preoccupation of philosophers today is that of a kind of *hyperanalysis* that distorts the natural realism of the human mind for seeing truth in its multi-dimensional reality. The habit of hyperanalysis leads to a kind of syndrome whereby the anatomized part of experience once dissected can no longer be visualized in relation to the whole. It is a habit of mind that leads to a *loss of meaning* because of a preoccupation with "the meaning of meaning" and because of the failure to know that the meaning of human experience cannot properly be divorced from the *content* in which it is found. Accordingly, if the true meaning of human existence is to be grasped at all it must be perceived dynamically and synthetically as part of the process of life itself. This is not to say, of course, that there is no place for linguistic and logical analysis in philosophy.

Such analysis in its proper context and development can play a positive and significant role. But it is against the abuse of analysis as a purely one-sided approach to philosophy, and the neglect of any other method that I take my stand.

In contrast, then, to the most obvious forms of such an

chapters Abraham Kaplan's, "The Travesty of the Philosophers," **Change In Higher Education** (January-February, 1970), Vol. 2, No. 1-2, pp. 12-19.

abuse what I am advocating is the development in philosophy of an integral realism that seeks to unite thought and action into a synthetic whole. Thought separated from action tends to distort the reality it is meant to convey even as action without thought tends to become irrational and blind. As for the habit of *hyper*analysis, we can only go so far with a minute and atomic examination of the syntactical elements of speech. At a certain point it becomes absolutely necessary to examine the realities themselves for which ultimately all human speech is intended as the vehicle of expression.

But this is not all. The remedy for the present situation is in part for philosophers to extricate themselves from the endless knots of those self-defeating epistemologies that have cut themselves off from the real world. The problem is that of emerging from the shadowy caves of subjectivism into the full light of day where realities are glimpsed, not as lifeless, dissected parts, but as living wholes. There is a need, in short, for a return on the part of philosophers to a true empiricism, in the best sense of the word, and not for a permanent confinement to the static empiricisms of the past.

The therapy therefore that is needed in philosophy today is in the way of a development of an integral realism that will lead philosophy away from hyperanalysis into a habit of mind that seeks an integration between action and thought such as was originally intended by the pragmatists. As I see it, the *strength* of pragmatism as a native development in American thought lies in its insistence on securing an inter-relationship between philosophy and life, but for reasons I hope to give later, the solution of the pragmatists was too short-ranged to be of permanent value. What is needed in the place of pragmatism today is a philosophy

60

that is dynamic, concrete, inductive, and, as I hope to show in the next chapter, open to the demands of a theological wisdom which is higher than itself, in short, a philosophy which is based on a radical empiricism of the spirit.

In a later chapter of this book I hope to show the true meaning of what I call a "radical empiricism." My own use of the term differs considerably from (though it also has something in common with) James' use of the term which he himself, incidentally, invented. My own theory of a true radicalism of the spirit (and I am hardly suggesting any kind of spiritualistic psychology) is based on the concept of a *variety* of layers of experience some of which lie below and others above the level of the rational and conscious aspect of human existence. It is further based on the contention that philosophers too often acknowledge—by reason of their exclusive commitment to purely rational methods of demonstration—only this surface level of experience, while ignoring all the rest on the grounds that these other levels (if they exist at all) are "outside their field." By contrast, the "radical empiricism" of which I speak is *in no way opposed* (as empiricism usually is in philosophy) to the reality of the transcendent, since it is the very element of the transcendent, preferably conceived in ontological terms, that gives human experience its highest and deepest meanings. The point I wish to make here against any of the forms of methodological dogmatism is that a true radicalism of the spirit is not only *not* reluctant to admit that there *are* different levels of experience, including what Maritain calls the "suprarational" (that, for example, of the poet and the mystic): it is desirous *by whatever means,* whether, let us say, by the method of introspection, of in-depth analysis, or even of the "method of crisis," of searching out the hidden realities that lie within these different levels as being the true measure of what is "really real" within the human psyche and of what lies beyond.

Finally, an authentic radicalism of the spirit as just described acknowledges that an understanding of these deeper levels of man's experience (so often denied by philosophers on *methodological* grounds) is not a matter for theologians alone, for "religious people" or for psychiatrists, but for philosophers who are willing to profess what Gabriel Marcel (1889-   ) calls a certain "humility before being." By the use of this expression I mean a right disposition of mind and will in relation to the deeper elements of human nature that somehow point the way, whether morally, metaphysically, or spiritually to the need of a Reality beyond itself. The true philosopher, in other words, is ideally, a man who is in search, not merely for rational proofs or logical arguments, but for whatever it takes and by whatever method to know reality on whatever level it might appear. He is a methodological pluralist all of the way and *in this sense* a true radical empiricist.

Where, then, is wisdom to be found? Clearly not in some simplistic form in the "drawers" of the past, but in a dynamic, living, and personal interpretation of the experience of mankind with respect to the ultimate nature of man. Such wisdom will express itself in a living philosophical tradition of the sort that disassociates itself from stagnant propositions to be learned by rote. Rather it is found in the expression of substantive truths about reality and in such ideas that can give one a whole new perspective in life.

So much for now of the need for a restoration of philosophy itself to a condition of well-being. Beyond this point, however, it is important to know that the philosopher himself, once restored to health, has strong obligations to society

at large. Most especially there is a need on his part, a profound need, to nurse the mind of contemporary man back
to a state of health, away from the debilitating diseases of
scepticism, agnosticism, and positivism. The natural realism
of the human mind must be restored to its former state if
there is to be any real advancement in the world of philosophy and in the world at large. The problem in short is to
reverse the enormous floodtide of a retreat into unreality
into a realism of the sort that will help to establish, pre-
eminently in the mode of the gospels, but to the inclusion
as well of all of the world religions, a radical continuity between man and his fellow-man and between man and the
rest of reality.

Addendum

Apropos of the modern problem, contemporary civilization is not lacking in heroic lives that are sacrificing themselves for God and fellow-man: witness the death in a Nazi
concentration camp of a Maximilian Kolbe who gave his
life in exchange for that of the father of a family, and witness the heroism of a Mother Teresa who administers to the
needs of India's poor. But that is hardly the point. The point
is that the inner dynamism of the socio-temporal order as
we know it today is unrelated either to the traditional wisdom of a philosophy which stresses the importance of man's
higher nature or the spirit of the gospels as such. If anything,
the orientation of world governments today is still in the
direction of pragmatism and, in many cases, in the direction
of a chauvinistic nationalism that disregards the true dignity
of other persons and other nations as having rights that are
inalienably their own. Given this, then, as the actual situ-

ation that exists in the world today, philosophers can play a vital role by responding to the challenge of exploring in depth those truths, realities, and principles that should be part of the patrimony of mankind. A philosopher as well as anyone else should be happy to profess, like Sallust, that nothing human is alien to his concerns.

5

MAN AND
HIS META-
PHYSICAL
NEEDS

*Introductory
Remark*

THE CONDITION
of modern man is all that the existentialists have said it to
be *and more.* A victim of scepticism, positivism, and agnosticism, man, as we know him today, wonders why he
should exist at all except in some blind and irrational sense
to "make the best of things as they are." Plagued by questions of ultimate concern, he has no way to search out the
answers to life except—in Sartrean fashion—to create *some*
project that will relieve his *Angst* but without giving him
the happiness he seeks.

In our last chapter we stated that modern man is a
problem to himself. To say this is to imply that man with the
tremendous expanse of his scientific and technological
knowledge—is in fundamental ignorance of his own real
needs. The basic question, then, is whether such ignorance
can be cured or not. If so, the situation—however depressing
it may appear—is not as bad as it seems.

The central thesis of this book is that such ignorance
can be cured. There is no need in supposing—as it has been
supposed for hundreds of years—that self-knowledge is

unattainable. As a matter of fact it is, but the proper remedy does not lie in the direction of scepticism, positivism, and agnosticism. It lies rather in the development of a *realism* that takes fully into account *all* that man is in terms both of his material and spiritual endowments. If indeed philosophy is to play any role at all as therapy, then it is necessary for present-day man to regain a sense of realism about himself, about God, about his fellow-man. None of these convictions, however, can be restored on a practical basis unless philosophy itself is restored to a condition of sound health.

Philosophy and the Cult of Unwisdom

In my first attempt at visualizing the scope and direction of this book I had imagined philosophy in the United States to be at a crossroad. Yet as time went on and with further reflection the conviction grew that philosophy has reached, not a crossroad, but, as a very perceptive friend of mine has put it, a *cul de sac,* a dead-end street. The obsessive influence over the post-war years of linguistic analysis as an exclusive method of philosophy has, in this author's opinion, put a halt, not only to philosophy as we have known it in the past, but to the very idea of philosophy as an attempt to search out the meaning of life.[1]

1. The point of my remarks is this: In the past many philosophers have attempted to conduct, whether in the manner of rationalists or empiricists, a search for wisdom. Whether in each case the search was successful or not is a question for history to judge. Yet the fact remains that men so widely different as Spinoza and James had thought that philosophy should have something to do with life, whereas this conviction no longer holds. With the possible exception of existentialism, phenomenology, and neo-thomism the pursuit of philosophy as wisdom has come to a halt, and instead we have witnessed a retreat into a predominant

Man and His Metaphysical Needs

The present state of philosophy is a situation any good historian of ideas could have predicted if he were sufficiently versed with the causes of its decline. These causes reach back to the very beginning of the classical modern era and continue to exert their influence on philosophy today. Witness, for example, the repeated attempts, especially in the British schools of philosophy to reduce philosophy to sense data, to mathematical principles, to the egocentric predicament, and in general to the whole syndrome of epistemology both in its classical modern and contemporary forms.

Here I do not obviously take a stand against epistemology as such, for this is an integral form of all philosophical inquiry. But an obsessive preoccupation with the question of knowledge, and that within the framework of subjectivism, has led to the neglect of other vital areas of philosophical concern. While science, then, was making unprecedented strides in opening up new avenues of knowledge, philosophy as wisdom of life has suffered a near total eclipse that has led to positivism in a wide variety of forms. *Scientific* positivism has asserted in effect that there really are no ultimate truths, only immediate ones of the sort that are served by the use of "scientific" method—as if scientific method were all of one piece. *Logical* positivism has set forth the claim that the work of philosophy is not to pursue the "dim nonsense" of metaphysics, but a clarity either of logical or grammatical structure that will prove all questions

if not exclusive concern with what Mortimer Adler has called "second-order questions," while those of substantive concern are ignored. As I see it, the real need is that of a contemporary revival—in some new form— of the wisdom tradition in philosophy or a reconstruction in philosophy—that will carry us beyond pragmatism, analytics, or even existentialism as we know it today.

of metaphysics to be ultimately nonsensical and therefore irrelevant. Finally, *sociological* positivism has taken the stand that all values are purely utilitarian expressions of what any given society or culture *wants*, not of what it fundamentally needs, there being nothing in the nature of man that gives rise to a set of values that are valid for all men.[2] In general to the extent that positivism has had its way, philosophy is no longer a wisdom that is sensitive to the needs of the spirit, but a narrow specialization, a technique, that confines itself for the most part to questions of method alone.

Kant and the Illusion of Metaphysics

Few works have had such a profound influence on modern thought as did the writings of David Hume, especially his *Treatise on Human Nature*. Hume's intent was to restore philosophy along the lines of a "science" of human nature that would make it possible for man to understand himself through the method of a thoroughgoing empiricism. Even in his own eyes, however, the "experiment" Hume had projected had failed not, as he saw it, because of an inadequacy of method, but because of the radical incapacity of the human mind itself to know anything beyond sense data. The result of all this was not that Hume as an original thinker had made no contribution to philosophy as indeed he had, especially through his laws of association

2. The three forms of positivism I have just traced out often blend with each other. For example, Harvey Cox's volume, **The Secular City,** represents a blend of its own of scientific and sociological positivism as is typified by the author's criticism of classical theism on the grounds that "it needs some ultimate explanation of reality," of which apparently the author does not approve. See **passim,** Chapter 11, "To Speak In a Secular Fashion of God," **The Secular City** (New York: Macmillan Company, 1965).

and his ethics of benevolence, but that his epistemology
had led him to a dead-end street. To appreciate the significance of this last remark understand that great philosophers like Hume are often praised by their successors, who
inherit their mistakes, for the wrong reasons, while their
real and positive contributions often lie fallow for centuries.

About the time, then, that Hume himself had lost all
abiding interest in philosophy, Immanuel Kant (1724-1804)
who had read Hume's *Treatise* had—on his own testimony—
been "awakened from his dogmatic slumbers." The "dogmatic
slumbers" of Kant were the slumbers of a dogmatism that
was rooted in the highly rationalistic interpretation of
metaphysics that characterized one of his earlier mentors,
Christian Wolff (1679-1754). Metaphysics to Wolff was
the ambitious study of the whole of reality with precious
little regard for any intellectual modesty that would bow
to a realm of mystery beyond itself. As against such a view
Kant, after reading Hume, was convinced that the Wolffian
interpretation of metaphysics, and for that matter the only
one with which he was intimately familiar, was a grotesque
pretension and at best an idle dream. Given, then, the need
for a reconstruction in philosophy that might deliver it from
the sensationalism of Hume, Kant set about the momentous
task of re-interpreting philosophy, not as metaphysics, but
as "criticism." In this view "dogmatism" was no longer a
viable position and the great need now was to reconstruct
philosophy anew along the lines of a doctrine of *a priori*
forms.

This doctrine is a pedagogical stumbling block to anyone
who is not a professional philosopher, but what it amounts
to is this: the mind in its confrontation with "reality" is in
no way "exposed" as it were, to an objective reality exactly
as it appears to be; rather the "world" as we know it is the

combined result of outside appearances that are *given* and of certain preestablished molds which the mind itself *superimposes* on the *phenomenal* contents of experience. In a word, it is the mind itself which supplies the basic forms or molds by which we interpret "phenomena" (appearances) through such subjective, though universally operative, categories as time, space, and substance.

The effect of the Kantian critique was to declare that reality is never what we imagine or conceive it to be, but the result of our own interpretation of it in terms of the universal forms of the mind itself. At this point of our analysis let me suggest that there were many respects in which the Kantian critique of knowledge was unquestionably right. No one, for example, can deny that in the very act of perception we do inject our own interpretation into experience and likewise in regard to conception: in our attempt to conceptualize objects, we do so, not in abstraction from the categories of our own experience, but always (and more so than we realize) from a certain *point of view*. In other words, the consciousness of the individual, laden as it is with the background of many past individual and social experiences, is always part of the "given" in any concrete act of human cognition. To Kant therefore more than to anyone else credit must be given for the full and explicit acknowledgment of this fundamental truth.

Yet acknowledging the above for the original contribution that it represents, we must also acknowledge that the effect of the Kantian critique was to deny the fundamental objectivity of *all* the categories of experience, such as substance, action, and cause. In other words, the effect of the Kantian critique was to have pressed the point of his original discovery to the very breaking point of denying the intelligible structure of being itself. So much for the basic position of

70

Kant. What is important to know is the measure of influence this doctrine has had on the world as we know it today. The influence of which I speak is this: under the impact of the Kantian critique few philosophers, including the pragmatists, are realistic enough in their outlook to agree that we can and do know the intelligible structure both of man himself and of the world in which he lives or to admit that there is any intelligible reality at all. Knowledge about reality is for these philosophers no longer, as it once was thought to be, an intelligible grasp into the nature of the real, but only an encounter with appearances. From this point on, all that man can do at best is attempt to establish a correlation of appearances. No doubt Kant himself would be surprised—immeasurably so—were he to know the extent of his "Copernican" revolution in philosophy, but in a sense the personal expectations of the author of this doctrine, that is, of the priority of mental forms over the world of matter, are quite beside the point. What is to the point is the question of knowing that the Kantian position, whether accepted in its original form or not, has paved the way, *against the best intentions of its author,* toward a radical subjectivism in philosophy which holds that the mind is no longer open to reality but the other way around: "reality," as we seem to know it, is the result of the pre-determination of the mind. This means that consciousness is no longer a medium for intuiting the real, but a medium whereby the knower approaches reality with his own set of categories and in so doing interprets, in the very act of knowing, not reality, but the *appearances* of the real according to the intrinsic limitations of his own mind. Kant in other words, had set up through his doctrine of forms, and against the best traditions of realism in philosophy, a sort of smokescreen between mind and reality of the kind that disallowed any ultimate insight

71

either into the nature of things or into the nature of man. Accordingly, noble as was Kant's attempt to establish on absolute grounds a true system of ethics (and there is much in his system that is *profoundly* true), the only possible approach to the world of values after Kant was by way of some kind or another of imperative. This means that that which is good for man is so, no longer because man recognizes it to be inherently good on ontological grounds: rather the ultimate justification of the good lies in what man himself determines to be good *through his will.* This obviously is not Kant's own position, but the *effect* of the split he created between pure and practical reason was to throw open the door to a host of anti-intellectualist philosophies that did assert against the value of reason *in any form* the absolute primacy of will.[3]

Lest the point of the inquiry be lost for all of the positive implications it is meant to convey, let me state my own basic hypothesis of integral realism as follows: the work of philosophical reason or intelligence is less that of *creating* meanings or superimposing them on the supposedly "phenomenal" contents of experience, as it is that of interpreting what is meaningfully signified, that is, in an objective way

---

3. Later in this volume I shall say more of the voluntarisms that have infiltrated the thinking of man as we know him today. Suffice it to mention here that there is a definite line of continuity between one type of will-oriented philosophy and another. In Schopenhauer, for example, we find a radical emphasis on the will to exist; Nietzsche's philosophy points up the will to power; James's, the will to believe; and the psychology of Freud, the will to pleasure. Only in very recent times has there fortunately been a discovery by Viktor Frankel of the will-to-meaning. This latter concept, however, has been overlooked by philosophers, and to this day a split exists between positivists, and sceptics, on the one hand, and the life-philosophers, on the other, all of whom give primacy to the dynamics of will. The great need here is for bridging the gap in philosophy between intellect and will.

within experience itself. Experience (considered thus in fundamentally *objective* terms) is pregnant with meaning, value, importance, or what have you, presuming, of course that one has sufficiently trained himself (to use a favorite Deweyan expression) to this kind of "logic of inquiry." I, for one, cannot reconcile my own understanding of the given in experience with the attempt, whether by Kant, Dewey, or the neo-existentialists to *superimpose*, or to *project* or to *create* that which is essentially a matter of discovery and response. In other words, the basic values of experience, especially those that fall within the domain of natural law, are such that, although they become values only for those of us who are prepared to accept them, are nonetheless founded in the objectively real contents of experience.

What I want to stress, then, as to the world of values, is the need for an integration (which Kant himself failed to secure) on an *objective* level between reason and the *whole* of experience. Whereas the problem exists for Kant of an inauthentic disjunction between reason as a quasi-autonomous faculty and the "thing in itself," a true integral realism suffers from no such prejudice of the mind but attempts instead to view reason within the total framework of a genuinely human experience. This much then, for the epistemology of Kant and the influence that it had on the ethics of those who, willingly or otherwise, had placed themselves under its spell. As for the question of metaphysics, there is no doubt that the influence of the Kantian critique was to deny—under the aegis of the faulty model of Christian Wolff—that true metaphysical knowledge of reality was possible. Yet in fairness to Kant it should be stated quite clearly that he himself never denied that man has a *need* of metaphysics. In Kant's own view man could not avoid asking metaphysical questions though he was equally insistent in affirming that the answers to those questions could be given on the basis of practical reason alone.[4]

Relative to the status of philosophy in the United States today, the point is not to show that there are any or many disciples of Immanuel Kant, but rather to point out the negative impact of his transcendental critique which consisted precisely in the rejection of any claim to a metaphysical wisdom that goes beyond the psychological categories of the mind. Consciousness itself is for Kant (through the mediation of his *a priori* forms) the ultimate determining factor of anything that we claim to be real, and the influence or *effect* of this doctrine is especially manifested in the fundamental postulates of pragmatism. None of the pragmatists, of course, accepted the doctrine of the *a priori* forms in its original formulation or intent. But what they did accept, especially James and Dewey, was *the principle that the determining source of our knowledge was not the "given" as such, but our own personal and social needs*. It was these very needs which, so to speak, played the role in the pragmatist noetic that the *a priori* forms played in the noetic of Kant. Accordingly, and in such a view, it is ultimately I myself (either as an individual or as a member of society) who *makes* things to be true, which is to say, in the language of Dewey, that my own felt needs are the determining source both of the direction of all inquiry as well as its final goal. So much, then, for the history of the matter. The issue

---

4. It is a point, therefore, in Kant's favor that he should at least insist on the **necessity** of raising these questions—even though (from the standpoint of his philosophy) there is no effective way of providing their answers. Note, then, the contrast between Kant's view and the positivists who have followed in his path: The positivists (of whatever sort) go far beyond Kant in their refusal to allow that such questions have any meaning at all. To them metaphysics in **any** form is nonsense. To Kant it is not.

now is whether and in what sense the need, indeed, the hunger, for metaphysics, as recognized by Kant himself, continues to this day.

A Re-Statement of the Question

No doubt many persons these days are bewildered by the strange sounding name of "metaphysics" as it might signify to them some kind of spiritism, a claim to preternatural knowledge, or even a theosophy of sorts. In no such mistaken sense as this, however, do I speak of metaphysics in this chapter. Nor does reference to the question as to whether man has a metaphysical hunger in any sense imply that all men have an innate capacity for becoming professionally involved in the "science of being as such." My only initial intent rather is to ask whether it is possible for man to conduct his life in a state of complete indifference concerning questions of ultimate concern. Thus in its minimal sense, and in a sense that Kant himself would admit, to be "metaphysical" means to express a concern—in some way or another—for the ultimate meaning of life. Does life have a meaning that extends beyond the immediacies of our ordinary everyday experience or are questions of this sort totally irrelevant to man as we know him today?

Perhaps some persons would grant at the outset that man cannot help raising questions of ultimate concern. Yet, allowing this to be so, they might go on to argue—as would a sociological positivist, that the habit of so doing is the result of centuries of conditioning along the lines of a purely non-scientific approach to the problem of man in the world. In other words, and this would seem to be the thinking of Harvey Cox in *The Secular City,* man is so much a product of his training and environment that even the questions he asks about himself, including those that seem most basic, are an expression, not of the human condition as such, but of the human condition as it is localized in time and place. Man in this view is totally a product of his social and cultural environment.

While it is not my intent at this moment to conduct a full-fledged analysis of sociological positivism, I think it is relatively easy to point up a few factors that seem rather damaging to the hypothesis that was paraphrased in the paragraph above. For example, why is it that men from a wide variety of cultures and backgrounds, are often prone —given their fundamental failure to resolve in some positive way the basic problems of life—to commit suicide? Quite often persons in the best of health and with large financial endowments regard their lives (for no earthly reason) as a failure—even to the point of destroying themselves. Surely, suicide is not such a widespread phenomenon that men and women whose lives are otherwise marked by apparent success will commit this act out of caprice. Nor will anyone in his right senses concede that suicide itself (like all other values!) is so much a matter of convention that its practitioners will perform this act, as it were, from a sense of routine.

Yet apart from the extreme case of suicide, is it not more fundamentally the case that men often pause to ask themselves *why* they are living rather than not? Is it merely the case that they are culturally determined to do so, as it were, out of a sense of compulsion, duty, or routine, or, do they *freely* ask this question because there is none they consider more basic—more basic than food, clothing, sex or any of their other biological needs? Offhand, few questions seem to have less routine significance than that of one's purpose in life. But rather than argue the point, let us pause to consider that *man is the only kind of being we know of who does in fact ask such ultimate questions.*

He wants to know, not merely from the point of view of himself as a carpenter, teacher, or a lawyer, but whether from the standpoint of himself *as a man,* if his life is really a failure or a success. Why this is so, namely that man is the *only* being we know of who raises this sort of question, may not at all be clear, but the fact of the matter is that he does—and does so in such a manner *as to give an absolute priority to this over all other questions.* As to whether one's marriage or business is a success, all other such questions of whatever degree of importance, pale by comparison with the question as to whether one is successful, not *in* life, but *with* life itself. Further, it would be absurd even to try to imagine a horse or a dog developing a neurosis, even to the point of suicide, over the question as to whether or not it is fulfilling its purpose in life. Yet such is the case with reference to that unique creature we call "man."

When we state therefore that man has a metaphysical hunger we imply many things in this one simple statement, but first and foremost that man has a radically different attitude *toward himself*—than does anything else that we know of. Too, the fundamentally metaphysical character of human existence may be gathered from the fact that man is the only being we know of who under given conditions is in need of a psychiatrist. I am not suggesting, of course, that all men are in need of psychiatrists, but that there exist enough of them who do to lend truth to the proposition that the psychosomatic nature of man gives rise to disorders no other animal is capable of. Neuroses of all sorts and the conflicts that underlie them are an unfailing clue to the fact that man has needs, cultural, spiritual, and moral needs that totally transcend every aspect of his biological side. The "problem of man," then, is not simply the problem of how to *maintain* one's existence, but of how to give it meaning in the first place. It is a problem of giving a mark, a character to one's existence in terms of a purpose that transcends our biological needs.

Given, then, the complexity of our nature, I should be quite willing to concede with Sigmund Freud (1856-1939) the harmfulness of our repression of the demands of the *id*. What Freud overlooked, however, is the yet greater damage that results from the suppression of our spiritual ideals. To use Freud's own language, he failed to see that the "superego" has certain demands of its own that totally transcend those of the "id" which it sublimates. Talk to anyone whose life is "ruined" by the failure of the past, real or imagined, and you will find that such a person has employed in one fashion or another a method of escape from his "existential neurosis." On the other hand, most honest persons are perfectly willing to assume the responsibility both for their failures as well as for their successes. Few persons, however, are capable of such a high degree of honesty in the absence of which they spend half their lives trying to "justify" what they otherwise know to be the mistakes of the past, their failure to measure up to their own ideals.

Modern Life and the World of Make-Believe

Having given some evidence of the metaphysical nature of man, whether various philosophers admit it or not, we must further explore what this means. The unprejudiced reader will no doubt agree with what we have been saying, but the question that lurks in his mind is "Where do we go from here?" As a starter I would suggest the necessity of getting beyond pragmatism and existentialism. Certainly, pragmatists are right in suggesting the necessity of measuring the value of a course of action by its consequences. But the question they leave unanswered is this: How to produce the consequences that give evidence of interiorly happy lives? Existentialists too are right, entirely so, in pointing up the reality of human *Angst*, but where do they provide any satisfactory means for its ultimate relief? Existentialists feed on *Angst*, but a man who has no other experience to go on will ultimately go insane. So the problem again is this: What can philosophy do to lead modern man to a condition of health?

While I intend within the various chapters of this book to suggest some remedies that are needed, I submit that the very first step that must be taken is that of a proper diagnosis of the disease itself. No doubt it is an over-simplification to speak in the grammatical singular of the "disease" of modern man; man today suffers from *many* diseases. Yet there is a single source from which all of these diseases develop and that is the failure to face up to the problem, indeed, the mystery, of his existence.

Consider, for example, the restlessness of modern life. Why is modern man restless? Is mobility such a fundamental goal in life that one should pursue it, as it were, for its own sake or as an end in itself? Clearly, restlessness of any sort is, on the surface of things, a sign of dissatisfaction with the *status quo*, and in one sense, an indication of a desire to progress. But this is not my meaning of the term. The restlessness of which I speak is a fundamental dissatisfaction with one's existence as such. It is characterized, not by the pursuit of superior goals in terms of the fulfillment of one's nature, but by the pursuit of an ever increasing desire to try new solutions to the problems of life where all others have failed. The man, for example, who marries five wives (presumably in rather rapid succession) more likely than not imagines with each new wife that *she* will be the answer to his life's problems. What he fails to see is the fact that the problem lies, not with his wives, but with himself.

All of this is to say that neither pleasure (whatever form it may take), nor power, nor wealth, nor fame can of themselves provide any ultimate solution to the problems of life. The ultimate solution, if it is to be found at all, must be looked for from within, in terms of the inwardness of one's own being, and not in terms of what some classical philosophers have designated as "external goods" whether in terms of number of wives, sailboats, executive positions, money, and fame. These latter accentuate with a certain kind of irony the "wound of existence" if the fundamental problems of life remain unsolved.

So much for a statement of principle. As for the fact of the situation let me say this: many aspects of life as we know it today are in total disharmony with the nature of man as *he is*. What with all the emphasis on secondary needs, many of them being the contrived needs of the ad man, modern man has been sold on the proposition that the only thing that matters is, not *why* you are living, but *how* you are living in terms chiefly of the material conditions of life. Rightly have the hippies and all other social dissidents suspected that there is something essentially "phony" in regard to such an attitude toward life. Thus it is one thing for children to build castles in the sand and cities out of blocks, but quite another for adults to dream themselves into a world of their own making when the real world—not of material things as such, but of their own spiritual existence—goes by the board. The problem, then, with many adults in our present-day society is that they literally live in a world of make-believe. The categories which dominate their thinking are categories drawn, not from an understanding in depth of the problems of life, but from the idyllic dreams of their own creative imaginations, from what Francis Bacon has depicted as the idols of the cave, of the market place, and the tribe. Carl Jung (1875-1961) has spoken of a "collective unconscious." By an extended application of his term one might say that modern society too suffers from the "collective unconscious" of its own delusions in the absence of any clearcut perception of the fundamental goals of life.

All of this, of course, gets us back to the basic proposition that modern man, in spite of his self-made delusions and in spite of the subjective categories of his own mind, suffers withal from a neurosis that is not curable by the methods of psychology alone. Although psychology may relieve the symptoms of these characteristically modern disorders, it is the work of philosophy as integral realism to manifest the cause. The fundamental cause then, of the disorders of modern life lies in man's failure to face the very problem of existence itself. The world of make-believe as modern man has constructed that world for himself, in a myriad of forms, is a world that would do justice to the "als ob" ("as if") philosophy of Friedrich Schleiermacher (1768-1834). The great lie of modern life is the elaborate and futile attempt to go on living "as if" matters of trivial concern, like the brand of toothpaste you use, were of greater importance than the meaning of life itself. As Viktor Frankl has rightly pointed out, there is nothing more fundamental than the will to meaning. To choose to ignore this fact is, to put the matter in the most quaint and euphemistic terms, to create a disturbance in the soul.

Existential Neurosis: What Does It Mean?

In the metaphysics of Jean-Paul Sartre existence itself,

human existence, is a neurosis, a kind of disease. Merely to exist, is for him, to be afflicted with a disease that one can only hope to alleviate, not to cure. On this point I find a great similarity between the pessimism of Schopenhauer and that of Sartre. For both of these men the problem is not so much that of confronting objective reality in its own terms, but of creating rather a method of escape, a project that can at best serve as a means of distraction from the fundamental "disease," even the absurdity, of our existence. Little wonder, then, that Sartre should feel the need to *apologize* for existence, as though to exist for man, absurd as it may appear to be, instead of being a blessing, were a curse.

The reason no doubt why existence is for Sartre a burden, not a joy, lies in the fact that for him it has no orientation toward a goal. In fact the only goal we can speak of at all is the one that each man arbitrarily determines for himself. Unquestionably Sartre is quite right in showing that there is "no exit" for man, given his hypothesis as to the radical absurdity of our existence. But is the hypothesis true? From a purely empirical point of view is it not the case that many people are truly quite happy with the fact that they do exist and that they do so *in a meaningful way.* Thus it would appear that the meaningfulness of existence, as an ideal if not as an accomplished fact, is evidenced by the real capacity that many persons have for transcending themselves. To cling to one's existence as though in total isolation from everything else that exists is, of course, to distort the meaning of one's existence or, what is worse, to find no meaning in existence at all. But for many persons this is not actually the case. Contrary to the generalizing tendencies of John-Paul Sartre, many persons do find their existence meaningful insofar as they can through a measure of self-transcendence serve some cause beyond themselves. As to the question of whether life itself is a neurosis, let me say this: a neurosis *of any sort* is a symptomatic disturbance indicating an inner conflict in one's life, and given this to be so, it is quite possible for a person to feel that the very character of his life is like a disease. However, it would appear that Sartre is too quick to generalize from the limited experience of *some* who feel that life, *their* life, is a failure to the supposition *that it must be so for the whole of mankind*. Accordingly, not all men feel, as Sartre seems to think (and Schopenhauer before him) that there is a need for *escape*. In fact, many persons are fully persuaded that there are some values in life, including human existence itself, that do have an objective basis in the nature of things. They are further convinced that through the exercise of their freedom *and their intelligence* they can realize these values, like the love of their fellowman, in their personal lives. In a word, if I may paraphrase a saying of Mark Twain's, the report of the moral death of many individuals in our society today is "highly exaggerated," and there is definite room both within human nature itself and within some of the conditions of modern life for a philosophy of hope. To conclude this section of our chapter, let us say that we are indebted to Sartre for giving us in his *No Exit* a dramatic portrayal of a modern hell which in many respects surpasses Dante's *Inferno*. Yet the picture Sartre represents, of people hating each other as objects that exist in total isolation from each other, may not be as universally valid as the playwright's imagination makes it out to be.

Can Metaphysics Function as a Therapy?

Let us take it for granted at this stage that there is

4

something fundamentally metaphysical about the nature of man that is in no way characteristic of other living things, and that man is the sort of being who pauses, at least on occasion, to ask metaphysical questions, whether he recognizes them to be so or not. Now I want to move on to ask the reader to consider whether metaphysics can in some way function as a therapy. This question may be difficult to resolve because it is fraught with ambiguities that may not be easy to overcome. Yet let us try at least to clear the way toward an understanding of the issue at hand. In one sense metaphysics is not, nor was it ever intended to be, a therapy insofar as it represents to many professional philosophers a purely speculative kind of knowledge that is not *per se* ordered to any kind of use. The value of such knowledge is considered to be an end in itself, and its justification lies, not in any practical use, even as therapy, but in the measure of intellectual satisfaction it affords. Yet allowing this to be so, I would call the reader's attention to another factor which is this: Quite often the most "useless" sort of knowledge, independently of the intention of the knower, leads to the most fruitful results as is frequently the case when a scientist whose motives are "pure" makes a sudden discovery of how his knowledge can be put to practical use.

Let us allow, then, that although metaphysics is not *per se* useful—it may turn out to be more useful than much so-called practical knowledge. Yet the mere possibility does not establish the fact so I am still faced with the burden of proof to show that metaphysics can somehow serve as a therapy. Obviously I am not at this point suggesting that everyone should become a metaphysician, nor that metaphysicians do not themselves have practical problems to face that can be resolved by metaphysical means alone. But what I do mean to suggest is that metaphysics can and should serve as a kind of wisdom that represents for those who possess it both a high level perfection of their intelligence as well as an overall view of reality that gives them a perspective in their personal lives. Metaphysics if indeed it is fulfilling its proper function brings the intelligence of the knower into a direct and vital contact with the truth of things, which is to say, with the deeper levels of truth as they exist, not in our imaginations, but in the real, objective world.

In a moment I shall return to the question of how metaphysics, or at least the incipient metaphysics that is implicitly contained in the judgments of common sense, can somehow serve as a therapy. Yet I want to return to the point, however briefly, that the rejection of an objective metaphysics has historically deprived modern man of a natural wisdom that is his due, and this, at a time in human history when he is most desperately in need of such knowledge. Nor can it be stated often enough that once the human intelligence is deprived of its own proper good—which is the knowledge (on many different levels) of the *truth*—man himself is left at bay to make options, whether by way of a categorical imperative or not, that fail to harmonize with his nature. This is to say that the judgments of our human intelligence, if they are truly based on what is most deeply true in man and reality, can form the basis of a genuine human freedom. Freedom without intelligence is blind, and a categorical imperative with no adequate basis in the speculative order to justify it can only lead to contradictory results. This is to say that if morality has no properly objective foundation that is discernible to man's natural intelligence, it could easily happen that one man's virtue could become another man's vice.

Allowing, then, that not every man is called to be a metaphysician, it is nonetheless true that every man should choose his life's options on the basis of what is grounded both in the truth of his own human nature and in the truth of the world, not only as he sees it subjectively, but in the truth of the world as it exists in itself and in its relation to God as its Primary Cause. As to this last point we should note that the knowledge of God as Primary Cause can be acquired either on purely natural grounds, as through a proper method or philosophical demonstration, or it can be acquired supernaturally through what we might call the "method" (though it is much more than that) of an objectively grounded religious faith that is based on a divine revelation.

In any event, while a formal knowledge of metaphysics is hardly a pre-requisite to a good moral life, it is nonetheless true that a truly *rational* morality should be grounded in the nature of things as they are, and not merely as we imagine them to be.

Metaphysics, then, can serve as a kind of therapy that places us in contact with the truth of things, with what the old scholastics would call *veritas rerum* and it is this *veritas rerum* which once properly seen or visualized by the human intelligence, whether by the method of strict metaphysics or not, can serve as the basis for directing our lives along the right path. What, then, is the tragedy, be it only intellectual, that results from the failure to give metaphysics its day in court? Quite simply this: that the human intelligence—as an instrument, not primarily of control, but for knowing the truth and that on many different levels—is deprived of its own proper good. And why is it important to know the truth? If only for the reason, as developed in an earlier chapter and as stated on the previous page, that our will is guided only by that which it knows. *False ideas lead to mis-*

taken lines of conduct, whereas true ideas usually lead to the opposite results.

Metaphysical vs. Technological Man

Before we conclude this chapter I should like to suggest the distinction that exists between metaphysical and technological man. By "metaphysical" man I do not necessarily mean the sort of person who knows metaphysics—but rather the sort whose ultimate purpose in life transcends his immediate concerns. He is the sort of person who acknowledges to himself, at least in his deepest moments, that life does have a meaning beyond his biological and technological needs. Such a person is obviously concerned with the problem of means and may even have a deep love of technology, but the means of life, as including everything from his razor to the aircraft he flies, are ordered and related to an end. This end may only be vaguely conceived and it need not even be couched in religious terms, but there is at least a recognition that man does have an end or goal that transcends his immediate concerns. Even the honest humanist who does not believe in God at least has a deep feeling of love and respect for his fellow-man—so that service to some higher cause is axiomatic to his way of life.

By contrast with the picture just drawn, "technological" man has no such acknowledged awareness of any transcendent goal. He is the sort of person who either denies or totally ignores that there is or should be any ultimate meaning beyond what we might call for him a "kingdom of means." As a tribute to Kant, for all of his disavowal of the objective character of metaphysics, we find at least a recognition of a "kingdom of ends." Not so, however, for those

87

technologists for whom the means are, as it were, their own justification. Nor should we ignore the fact that the general drift of our society lies in this direction of a preoccupation with means for their own sake. But any further comment on this subject should be reserved for a later chapter. Suffice it to say here that technological man has been pushed in the foreground and the hero of today is no longer in the image of the thinker of Rodin but in the image of the man who walks in his space suit on the moon. This is not to say that man should not widen his physical horizon, but that exploration in the world of outer space can easily become a meaningless venture if the world of inner space is ignored or denied. Fortunately, there is a growing minority of persons in our society who in however groping a fashion are beginning to explore this world of inner space—in the hope that they too will become re-oriented to what *is* rather than to that which *is not*. And on this point whether they know it or not they are happily taking the advice of wise old Parmenides who admonishes us to follow the path, not of illusion, but of being—of that which truly is.

Concluding Remark

Much more remains to be said about the metaphysical nature of man but suffice it in closing to suggest that there are three questions that all men should ask themselves whether they are metaphysicians or not: Where did I come from? Why am I here? Where am I going? All other questions are trivia by comparison.

6

THE
CENTRALITY
OF
PRUDENCE:
Notional and
Real Assent

*Introductory
Remark*

WE NEED NOT
apologize for the fact that philosophy—at least insofar as it
touches the real needs of real men—must be anthropocentric
and not merely linguo-centric as though its main concern
were with language and the problems of language rather
than with men and the problems of men. The need for
philosophy so understood is the need for developing some
kind of insight that will enable us to get at the underlying
causes, and not merely the symptoms, of the disorders that
plague the hearts of contemporary men.

The central task of this work, then, is to pave the way
toward a new approach to philosophy along the lines of a
radical empiricism of the human spirit. Such an empiricism
should be based, not merely on a contrived analysis of man's
knowing powers as such, but on a realistic estimate of the
totality of human nature. This task of understanding man in
his inner as well as in his outer dimensions is all the more
urgent because modern man has subjected himself to all
sorts of one-sided philosophies which are themselves the

reason why he has become a problem to himself. One of the great needs of our time, then, is the need of human intelligence to recapture the fullness of truth about human nature of the sort that will make men free. It is a pure illusion to think that modern man can save himself by science and technology alone, just as it is an illusion to think that philosophy too is the cause of salvation. There is, however, this redeeming feature of a sound philosophy, namely, that it can put man on the *path* to wisdom in its fullest sense.[1] As Josiah Royce (1855-1916) rightly insists, man is the kind of being who needs to be redeemed if only, in my view, from the many illusions he has created for himself. The tragedy of such myths and illusions—apart from their persistence—is the fact that they affect and determine the entire course of men's lives.

The Persistence of Ontological Questions

In our previous chapter we have tried to show that man is the kind of being who cannot avoid asking those ultimate metaphysical questions that relate to the meaning of life. Nonsensical as these questions may appear to many a positivist, the fact of the matter is that to the average person they are real. They are real, not in the contrived sense that man simply invents these questions out of whimsy or caprice; *they are real in the sense that no other questions are important by comparison.* To deny or repress such

1. By wisdom in its "fullest" sense I mean to suggest that view (representing a minority opinion in the eyes of my contemporaries) which accepts in a realistic manner the data of revealed truth on the basis of Christian faith. However, it is not this dimension (the faith dimension) which concerns me in the text, as much as it is my intent to point out the need for a natural wisdom.

questions is to cause immense psychological harm. And to ask them is to suppose (mistakingly or not) that some answer, if only a negative one, can be found.

Assuming, then, that man has profound metaphysical needs, we must proceed in this chapter to inquire as to the way or ways modern man should redirect the posture of his being to resolve the problem, indeed the mystery, of his existence. Let us begin by asking the following questions: Can modern man go on living as he does without an overall sense of direction and still preserve his sanity? Is it possible for modern man to go on ignoring the deeper implications of his life in the hope of escaping from his existential "neuroses" unscathed? Are such basic attitudes as pragmatism, situation ethics, scepticism, and so on in any way conducive to the ultimate solution of the problems of life? If not, in which direction should modern man turn? Further, what is the overall value of prudence in human life and how does one go about cultivating this virtue and why? These are some of the questions in the back of my mind as I continue to pursue with the reader the notion of philosophy as a type of therapy for the ills of our times.

Before we even attempt answering these questions we must reconsider the point that modern man is riddled beyond all self-diagnosis with a severe case of scepticism which is lack of confidence both in his own native powers of reason and in *any* source of knowledge that could constitute for him an area of revealed truth. The death-of-God movement, for example, such as it prevailed in the 60's, was, in my view, an indication of modern man's refusal to accept anything except in "empirical" terms of the kind of reality that transcends the limited witness of our senses. Positivism, whether in science, in philosophy, or in both, has led us to the belief that nothing—God included—can really exist unless it can in some way be verified by empiricism. But where lies the remedy to such an empiricism so narrow as this? Clearly not in the direction of the positivisms either of the past or the present which would resolve metaphysical questions by ruling them out of court. In the end there may be no ideal method of expressing man's metaphysical problems, but this is no warrant for denying the existence of the problems themselves.

As a matter of fact, our difficulty in expressing a problem is often a symptom, not of its non-existence, but of the depths from which it arises and the extent of the consequences to which it actually leads. Ask any parent for example, who has made an honest attempt to discover the problems of a teen-age daughter or son, and you will find that few of these problems, especially the deeper ones, are easy to bring to the fore. Few parents, however, will suffer the illusion that the problems themselves are non-existent. Likewise, then, with respect to those questions that pertain to the essence of life itself: From the fact that we find it hard to articulate the radical questions of our human existence, we should hardly infer that the questions are unreal or that we can forget about them by drowning ourselves in a sea of distraction. Personally, I find much more wisdom in the frank recognition of the fact that men do suffer from anxiety, neurosis, or what have you *because* of these problems.

Why Prudence?

To many persons prudence is an outmoded virtue insofar as it denotes to them a habit of unwarranted caution and nothing more. In this sense the prudent man is the bachelor who never leaps, the businessman who refuses to make investments and the athlete who will never take a chance.

The Centrality of Prudence

Needless to say, this is an altogether mistaken notion of what prudence is, but I am quite willing to let the matter rest at that. What concerns me greatly at the moment is the need for the practice of prudence in every phase and aspect of modern life. At every turn of the road modern man, will it or not, is faced with the problem of making decisions. However, this chapter is not concerned with prudence in the limited sense of "how to win friends and influence people," a narrow, pragmatic sort of prudence, nor do I mean by prudence a mere astuteness or cleverness in the conduct of one's daily affairs. Obviously, there is such a thing as the prudence of a businessman and of a military leader, of a politician and so on, but this is not what I have in mind. One can, for example, be an eminent success as a business man, but fail for want of prudence in the overall "performance" of his life. Prudence in its basic sense presupposes that a person has some understanding of the purpose of life itself. The prudent man is the one who conducts his activities in such a way that they are, all of them, ordered in relation, not merely to this specific end or that, but to the overall direction of his life.[2] Moreover, for such a person prudence means not only a well-ordered intellect, but a will that is properly disposed in relation to his "final" end. In this sense prudence implies, not just intelligence in its raw and abstracted state or condition, but intelligence conjoined with a well-ordered "appetite" for the "end." Why, then, is prudence necessary? For the simple reason that without it

2. The prosperity of psychologists in this country is conditioned in large measure by the loss of prudence as a controlling principle in modern life. The Greek and medieval notion of reason—practical reason—as a source of measure and balance for our human acts has to a large extent been either lost or abandoned. Spontaneity, impulse and passion have taken the place of order, purpose, and goal.

it is impossible for man to direct himself toward his "end" or goal, which is nothing else than his ultimate relation to God.

No doubt many persons will balk at the idea of committing themselves to a goal in life in the same way that some bachelors balk at the idea of getting married. Commitment to a goal implies in the thinking of some persons an encroachment on their freedom. Yet just the opposite is true: Unless we are committed to a goal we shall never discover what it means to be "free." A true freedom—in the deeper sense of a liberation of the human spirit from its possessions, prejudices, evil tendencies, or what have you—can be effected only to the extent that a person through deliberate choice has given a direction to his life through commitment to a goal; any other concept of freedom is an illusion. Accordingly, it is totally fallacious to imagine one is free only when he is relieved of commitment. Such "freedom" can only lead to boredom.

Unfortunately, few persons realize that the great source of unhappiness in their lives is due to a failure, not of good will, but of the intelligent exercise of their freedom in the way of prudence. What they fail to see is that a careful and consistent exercise of prudence can lead to a kind of happiness which many persons consider to be out of their reach. Contrariwise, the person who habitually gets himself into trouble, moral trouble, I mean, is the one who fails to act in a reasonable, well-directed way that will lead to satisfactory results.[3] A prudent man, then, is one whose moral behavior

3. Our concern is to show that prudence as a virtue is not the use of any means for the use of any particular end. To act in the first place toward an end that directly conflicts with the end of life itself is to act immorally, as when one wantonly kills a fellowman to escape with some stolen loot. Likewise, with the question of means; a prudent man is care-

94

is consistently marked by an ability to judge intelligently as
to the best course of action to be performed *with the result*
that he himself will be pleased with the consequences.

*Toward a Philosophy of Action: The Art of Making
Decisions*

The integral realism of which we have been speaking
in this book is a realism of the sort that achieves a practical
balance between thought and action. The problem with too
many philosophies is that they have either become too purely
"intellectual" in the sense of confining themselves to endless
processes of analysis or too purely voluntaristic in the sense
of failing to seek adequate guidelines as the basis of intelligent action. Realism seeks to integrate within a single
philosophy the best elements both of thought and of action.
What, then, are the ingredients of a realism that leads to
prudent action? On a very general level, I would suggest
three things: *memory, presence of mind,* and *foresight*. Without memory it is quite impossible to establish any continuity
in one's life. A person, for example, who suffers from amnesia finds himself in all sorts of predicaments that are impossible either for him or anyone else to explain. At every
turn of the road he finds himself in "hot water." The need
for memory, then, is the need to reflect on one's past experiences for the making of future decisions. Yet the making of
wise decisions requires something more than reflecting on
the past. It means knowing in the present whatever circumstances or events are relevant to the decision at hand.

ful, even to the point of being shrewd, to insure the moral rectitude of the
means that he uses for the execution of a good end. Robbing wealthy
merchants, for example, is hardly a suitable means for accomplishing
social reform.

95

Let us elaborate on this point a moment. Wisdom—the practical wisdom that is prudence—requires great care in "sizing up" a total situation. This means making a practical judgment as to what a person is capable of doing and what not; knowing all the relevant circumstances of time, place, persons, and so on, that are involved in the decision at hand. It is foolish, for example, for a person who is a good mechanic to dream of becoming a lawyer if he lacks the talent for a lawyer and has five children besides; and it is equally foolish for a person to accumulate a fortune if in doing so he ends up ruining his health. Unfortunately, however, many persons are the victims of this kind of foolishness whereby instead of living in the world of reality as it is, they choose instead to live in a dream world that carries them from one illusion to the next.

In this connection too, many persons are unmindful of the fact that they have only one life to live in the sense that the meaning of time lies, not in a ceaseless repetition of the mistakes we have made in our youth, but in a constant effort to move closer to the goal to which each of us is individually called or destined—both for our own personal good and that of our fellow-man.

Prudence, then, demands the constant exercise of an intense practical judgment that bases itself on a realistic estimate of our own capabilities and talents and the needs of our fellow-man. It means exercising *responsible* judgment as to the making of life-decisions, in all matters, great and small, in much the same way as a surgeon at the operating table is required—at a moment's notice—to make a responsible judgment as to the life and health of his patient. What we must see here is the intimate connection between prudence and *personal* happiness. Prudence, in other words, is not just a matter of judging about the past and the future;

it is a matter of working out in the present the one course of action that is best calculated to give meaning and direction to the course of our lives.

On the other hand, the failure to accomplish in the present moment what we judge to be the best for our lives—will result in the necessity of living with our mistakes. Not that it is possible to avoid *all* mistakes (no one is impeccable), but every attempt should be made—while the moment of opportunity exists—to act in a responsive and responsible way. Not to do so is to postpone a responsibility for our actions that we must face—if not in the present—then at some unhappy date in the future. The future consequences of our actions—once the action is performed—have a quality of being irreversible and irrevocable. No one can change the past, and once the act has been placed we are no longer free to accept or reject the consequences to which it leads.

So far we have spoken of the need for memory of the past and awareness of the present as conditions for prudential decisions. One last element remains: the need for foresight. Some people demand too much foresight, others little or none at all. To act prudently is not to demand that we know perfectly in advance the outcome of our deeds. Man, after all, lives in a contingent world in which the best laid plans "oft go awry." This failure, however, to know the future is no excuse for inaction, and a good measure of prudent action involves a great deal of risk.

The world, as it is often said, is based on hope—on the hope that having acted in a reasonable way we will not be "punished," as it were, for our best efforts but indeed merit their rewards. Even so, inability to know the consequences of our deeds does not relieve us of the necessity of making some practical estimate as to what those consequences might be. No man, of course, knows the future, but insofar as he

97

can surmise the future in its present causes a prudent man can reasonably discern where his actions will lead him, and to do this is to exercise foresight.

Prudence and Modern Society

As to the necessity of prudence: We must now see the relevance of this virtue to the problems of modern life. If we ask, for example, why the suicide rate in any particular society is as high as it is, the answer no doubt is to be found (philosophically) in the failure to exercise prudence.

To come directly to the point: modern society has become so absorbed in the problems of making a living that some persons, as we noted in our previous chapter, who have amassed veritable fortunes only to find no meaning in life itself. In extreme cases some persons have even thought it better to end their lives rather than go on living without any ultimate concern. The mistake here is a fundamental failure in prudence because of their preoccupation with the means of life coupled with a consequent failure to give attention to its end or goal.

The need, then, for prudence is identical with the need for recognizing *in fundamentally objective terms* the true and ultimate meaning of human life. It is inconceivable, in other words, that all of our secondary and derivative activities should be characterized by the ordering of a means to an end while life itself—in terms of an ultimate goal— should be meaningless and absurd. In point of fact, life *is* absurd for many people, not however, because there is no purpose or goal to be found, but because these same persons have mistaken proximate and derivative goals for ultimate ones. Success in business, reputation, good health, and the like, however desirable they may be from a human point of view, have a way of taking their revenge on the psyche if they are mistakingly identified as the ultimate object of happiness for man.

But let us get to the point at hand. Modern society is so oriented with its preoccupation as to the means of modern living that it has distracted man from his fundamental purpose in life. The existentialists have written well in their stress on the anguish of the human spirit but few of them have properly focused on the real cause—which is the false presupposition that man has no end outside of himself.

Prudence and the Philosopher

Throughout this volume I have emphasized that the work of philosophers is not so much to provide further and further analyses of the problems of human knowledge as such, but to integrate philosophy with life. Having spoken of the necessity of prudence, we are now in a better position to see how and why this is so. In the first place it is impossible to a-chieve any kind of integration between philosophy and life until and unless philosophers give some measure of attention to the end or the goal of life, and to do this is to exercise prudence.

In this one important respect, therefore, I would submit that philosophy as we know it today has failed to provide for modern man the kind of therapy that is most needed with respect to the exercise of the most elementary kind of prudence, and we need not search hard for examples. Pragmatism, the kind of philosophy that has dominated the American scene, is rightly concerned with "consequences," ends, or goals, but only the limited goals of a narrow type of empiricism. What with all of his attempts, for example, to integrate philosophy and life, Dewey has never succeeded in showing that man is responsible for a goal in life other than those of his own making or choosing, To live in the fashion that Dewey prescribes is to move from one experiment in "democratic" living to another, but with no ultimate responsibility to a goal that lies outside of and distinct from the goals that society itself prescribes as its own "final" good.

The great challenge therefore to American philosophy today is that of paving the way toward a new approach to philosophy that goes beyond pragmatism as we have known it in the past. The positive merit of pragmatism as a philosophy of action is its recognition of the need for integration between philosophy and life; its central weakness is its failure to sustain a sense of purpose that goes beyond the limited goals of our immediate experience. Thus to teach children how to adapt to life is in itself a noble endeavor, but to fail to teach them what life itself is about is to leave them without any sense of direction.

Pragmatism, however, is not the only type of philosophy that has failed modern man. Marxism is equally at fault in providing for man a goal that is inconsistent with the totality of his human nature. True, Karl Marx was well enough aware of the need for philosophy to integrate itself with life: Yet the goals he provides fall far short of man's ultimate desire for meaning. Rightly did Marx consider the necessity of raising the level of the proletariat as no man can fulfill his purpose without economic means. Yet the goal of a classless society—in which all of one's economic needs are satisfied—is at best a one-sided goal. At worst it fails to provide for the reality of man's ultimate psychic and spiritual needs.

If we rightly interpret prudence in terms of practical wisdom, the same verdict that is made concerning pragmatism and marxism must be pronounced on the failure of existentialism to provide modern man with a sense of direc-

The Centrality of Prudence

tion that relates to the totality of his nature. True enough, some existentialists like Sartre would even deny that man *has* a nature, but the denial, it would appear, is contrary to the established facts. Sartre, for example, stresses the fact that man is at least capable of creating for himself a kind of freedom which to all appearances is inaccessible to horses, cats, or dogs, and if such be the case men (contrary to Sartre's hypothesis) do have something in common— whether we call it a common nature or not. My essential point, however, is this: What with all the emphasis on freedom existentialists have, by and large, failed to provide any solid direction to man's desire for transcendence. As I have pointed out elsewhere, existentialism, no less than pragmatism and marxism, is itself a form of voluntarism that fails to recognize any sense of purpose other than that which man superimposes upon himself.

On the basis of what we have said, the reader will no doubt acknowledge that the key point at issue is whether the exercise of prudence in an age of technology is a viable alternative or not.[4] To date science has not provided a sense

---

4. In the title of this chapter I have spoken of the centrality of prudence, and by this I mean to assert the basic and literal truth of the traditional doctrine that prudence must be at the helm of all the other virtues. Most of our contemporaries, of course, will wince at the idea of any virtue serving as directive principle of life, and the reason for this is their failure to know that the exercise of virtue—given the necessity of prudence—is equally a matter of intelligence, of practical intelligence, as it is that of a good will. As we have seen in our last chapter, it was the Kantian reduction of all morality to the categorical imperative that led modern man to a purely voluntaristic and to that extent also a subjective interpretation of what is morally good. Yet, contrary to Kant, it is necessary to admit in addition to a good will, an intelligent being who directs it to meaningful ends. For this reason too the Kantian axiom that there is nothing absolutely good except a good will is in need of serious qualification.

101

of direction because science does not concern itself with the question of ends or goals.[5] It would appear then, that the responsibility for providing some sense of direction in a technological age would devolve on the shoulders of philosophers. But where are these philosophers to be found? Surely not in the camp of those philosophers who completely demur from any sort of commitment to ethical or political goals on the grounds that the work of philosophy is restricted to the analysis of language and that alone. Nor, at the other extreme, can we find great consolation in all those schools of philosophy that *do* recognize the need for a goal but in a purely arbitrary fashion as does Sartre. For the latter there is no prescribable goal that is common to men by the very fact that they are men.

The great vacuum therefore that exists in our society is the utter poverty of a kind of intellectual leadership— wheth-

5. Here too we should recognize that all talk of means without goals is in any society, democratic or not, nonsensical. **Pace** John Dewey, the emphasis on an ever-changing society that is constantly in search of a greater and greater abundance of technological means takes man in the direction of chaos. Although it is unwise therefore for a philosopher or anyone else to prescribe any given set of arbitrary goals for any given society, it is the height of irrationality and unwisdom for that society to stress movement, freedom, change, for their own sake. The centrality of prudence, therefore, may be seen in any naive, simplistic interpretation of a kind of democratic freedom that knows no responsibility to the built-in goals of human nature itself. Indeed, every society should function (against the claims of a pure sociological relativism) to secure the common good of its membership and it should do so in a way that is commensurate with the ultimately rational nature of man. Prudence in the state, in society, means that the principle of reason, of a practical, directive reason, is in a position of dominant control over the irrational parts. Even as Plato recognized this in his day, so too must we in our own, namely, that a society dominated by the irrational part, by passion, by whimsy, by impulse or what have you, is one that is headed toward chaos, anarchy, and decline.

102

er from scientists, philosophers or both, to help it sustain a sense of direction at the time of its greatest need. Modern man's "sickness unto death" (to use a Kierkegaardian expression) can be cured in philosophical terms only by the development of an integral realism that recognizes the need for practical wisdom or prudence in the life of modern man. An integral realism in its turn is a philosophy of total human nature which fully acknowledges the reality of the subconscious depths of the human spirit and man's desire for self-transcendence. The repression of these radical tendencies in man leads to all sorts of psychological abnormalities and is the cause of many of the crises in society as we know it today.

Notional and Real Assent

Prudence, in the sense in which we have spoken of it, is too deeply a personal thing to be institutionalized and it is, in any case, the sort of thing that one can arrive at only through an intimate experience with life itself. Moreover, one does not come to be a prudent man overnight, but only as the result of a long and persistent attempt to establish a proper relationship between rightly considered ends and the means of their achievement. To sum up what we have said thus far: Prudence as practical wisdom means a reflection on the past, awareness of the present, and a practical orientation toward the fulfillment of future goals.

But this is not all. The most important part of prudence, and for that matter the part least often found among intellectuals, is the execution of the goal. Contrary to Socrates' hypothesis, the knowledge of the good as such is no guarantee of its fulfillment. Knowledge, in other words, is not the same thing as virtue, and if we are to speak at all of prudence as a virtue we must imply the actual fulfillment of the course of action we deem best.

Let us pause at this point to show the difference between what John Henry Newman has pointed out in terms of "notional" and "real" assent. Notional assent means that I can *see* or acknowledge the good of a given course of action but somehow I fail to do anything about it to make it a reality in my life. "Real" assent by contrast means that I not only see the good, but am properly disposed to do anything in my power to bring it about.

In the light of this distinction it is easy enough to see that the prudent man is not merely the one who "toys" with ideas, but is willing to act on them if he is convinced that they will bring him closer to his objective in life. He is the kind of person, in other words, who is capable of "real" assent. But let us deepen our understanding of this distinction. Take a student who is convinced of the need to prepare himself for his course. He is convinced (in the back of his mind) that he should do something about it, but instead procrastinates until the time of the final exam. At the time, however, when the professor announces the date of the exam the student no longer "toys" with the *idea* of studying. He is now *existentially aware* as to the immediate need for getting to the work at hand. In a similar fashion most persons go through life in a sort of dream world, realizing what they should do if they had the energy and the time, but failing for want of a strong enough motive to apply themselves to the task at hand.

The point of my making this distinction is to show that the condition of modern society is much the same as that of the man who is capable only of a "notional" assent. There is no want of dynamism, of course, in the pursuit of such prox-

104

imate goals as the success of one's business or profession, the selection of a marriage partner, the choice of a home or apartment, and so on. Yet when people, by and large, are faced with the problem of raising (in the manner of Hamlet) such questions as to why they exist at all they often prefer to go on *as if* these questions had no relevance to their lives. Admitting in some fashion that they will *someday* face up to the problems, they go on living their lives on the basis of "notional" assent.

Conclusion

It has always been a source of wonderment to me that there should be such a profound discrepancy between academic and real life. The reason, no doubt, may be found in the fact that the professor in the classroom feels that he can afford to detach himself from the issues of life—the very issues that burn in the depths of the consciousness of his students. The leading contention of this chapter, however, is to suggest that such a dicrepancy should never exist, least of all between philosophy and life. The restoration of a true and valid philosophy is dependent on a reconstruction of the sort that integrates the values both of intellect and will. Neither the "house of intellect" to use an expression of Jacques Barzun, nor of will taken by themselves are sufficient to provide a pathway for the life of man. Intellect by itself is powerless and will by itself is blind.

The real need, therefore, is for the development of an approach to a philosophy of action that consistently avoids the conflicts between "academic" philosophy and real life. In yet more positive terms, what we mean to stress is an integral realism of the sort that recognizes the centrality of prudence in human life as being the only adequate "method" for providing some sense of direction. Philosophical ideas have no meritorious quality of their own except and unless they bear some relationship to the life of a man, and for that matter also to his death.

7

EMPIRICISM:
HOW
RADICAL
SHOULD
IT BE?

*Introductory
Remark*

THE CENTRAL themes of this volume have been clearly established. Modern man is in a condition of "sickness unto death" and is in vital need of the kind of direction that can be had only from a valid and a sound philosophy. Yet, philosophy as we have known it in the past few hundred years has failed to respond to the real needs of society. Instead it has trailed off in the direction either of sterile logical analysis or in the direction of one kind or another of voluntarism. The problem therefore is the development of a new and enlarged type of philosophy that is relevant to the needs of our times. Such a philosophy I have designated as an integral realism.

Up to this point I have indicated some of the leading features of an integral realism. Integral realism begins with a wholesome confidence in man's ability to know *being*. He is not trapped, in other words, in the hopeless knots of a subjectivism that is fundamentally out of contact with the world as it is. A second feature of integral realism is that it is basically anthropocentric in its outlook, taking fully into account the totality of the nature we call "man." Thirdly, integral realism does not deal with man on either a purely rationalistic or on a purely voluntaristic basis: It seeks rather to emphasize the centrality of prudence in human life as a mode of practical wisdom. Fourthly, integral realism, in consideration of its anthropocentric character, is a philosophy that transcends the surface aspects of human nature to an understanding of all that man is in the depths of his being. Finally, (and this is the point of the present chapter) integral realism is a philosophy that is based on an enlarged understanding of the meaning of human experience. This means that integral realism is also a radical empiricism of the spirit.

The Meaning of Radical Empiricism

In the development of his own brand of radical empiricism William James placed his thought in sharp contrast with the associationist school of psychology initiated by Hume and carried to its climactic point of development by John Stuart Mill. James emphatically rejected any narrow concept of experience that reduced it to the level of discrete impressions and to the purely phenomenal correlation of events.

I myself am in fundamental agreement with James in his rejection of the empiricism of Hume and Mill. However, I shall attempt in the course of this chapter to show the limitations of James' own brand of empiricism and to give some hint as to the direction in which a new type of empiricism may be developed beyond the pragmatism of James, or, for that matter, of any other philosopher of the American tradition.

Let me begin, however, in a spirit—agreeable to that of

Empiricism: How Radical?

William James—with a critique of the scepticism of Hume and his followers. The entire method of "classical" empiricism in the tradition of Hume was to begin, not really with experience, but "ideas." The method, so to speak, was introspective from start to finish insofar as its sole object was to admit as valid only those ideas that were traceable to our *sensible impressions.* If, indeed, man had no sensible impression of himself, or of the outside world, or of cause, or of substance, there was reason to suspect according to the methodology of Hume that such "ideas" were furnished, not from without by the contents of experience, but by the workings from within of the imagination or reason, taken either singly or in combination with each other.

It is not my intent, of course, to become too technically involved in the empiricism of Hume, but the point is to show that Hume's own brand of empiricism was static, introspective, and did not in the first place begin with a real experience of what actually was given in the outside world. Rightly, then, did James as a realist criticize the empiricism of Hume on the grounds that the analysis of experience should begin, not with atomic ideas, but with an open recognition of the dynamism of our perceptual experience. Most of all did James insist, and rightly so, on the reality of relations as well as the reality of atomic events.

If all of this sounds mysterious to a non-professional philosopher the main point of James' insistence is this: Any empiricist deserving of the name should begin, not with a preconceived set of ideas, but with a certain openness of mind to the reality of experience itself. In its fundamental meaning therefore a "radical" empiricism—such as it was intended by James—is one that is "open" to any and all of the deliverances of our experiences whether they proceed from any internal or external source.

Limitations of the Empiricism of James

It would be a long chapter in itself to point out the merits of the new approach that James had contributed to philosophy. But to make a long story short, the value of his "radical" empiricism was his steady and consistent refusal to make any compromise with the positivism that prevailed in his day. When James, for example, delivered his famous series of Gifford lectures in 1901-1902 on *The Varieties of Religious Experience* he refused at the outset—and on methodological grounds—to make any compromise with a reductionist approach to the facts of religious experience.

Much the same, for that matter, could be said of the empiricism of Bergson, a great French philosopher, who himself exercised a strong positive influence on the philosophy of William James. Both of these men (Bergson in France and James in the United States) refused to adopt any "scientific" point of view that would in any way detract from the significance of the data of experience.[1] I mention the point here because of its relevance to the problems that philosophers face today. In the name of "empiricism" many of them have ruled out of court any commitment to a set of values that lie outside the range of a narrow "scientific" experience. To the credit, then, both of James and of Bergson no such restriction of method was ever a sufficient warrant for doing full justice to the facts.

At this point, however, it is necessary to speak of the

1. For an interesting study of the correspondence that developed between these two great philosophers see the various parts of the following book: R.B. Perry, **The Thought and Character of William James** (New York: Harper and Row, 1964). The book I cite is a condensed **Harper Torchback** edition of the one originally published in 1948 by Harvard University Press.

shortcomings of the "radical" empiricism of James. First in the field of psychology: Rightly did James criticize the old associationist doctrine of Mill in very radical terms. As James put it, Mill's attempt to account for the reality of the ego by means of associated impressions had reached the heights of a "paroxysmal unintelligibility" that was incomprehensible to Mill himself. Yet James' own stream of consciousness theory provided but little improvement over the doctrine of Mill. What it lacked most of all was a method of accounting for the ultimate reality of the ego or self as an ontological center of all our human activities as well as the subconscious depths of experience.

Let me try to clarify this point. According to James man himself is ultimately identical, not with himself as a living substantive unit, but with the state of consciousness that characterizes him at any particular moment. Each moment of consciousness subsumes, by some mysterious process, the reality of all of our previous states. How such a process comes about was never properly explained by James and the closest we can get to an explanation of the unity of our experience is James' hazy reference to memory as the vital link between our present and our past.

Concerning this stream of consciousness theory I have only this to say: It was not radical enough to account satisfactorily and along philosophical lines for the continuity of the self and for the experienced reality of the ego. True enough, Hume was right when he said long ago that I can never literally catch "myself" apart from my conscious states, but he was wrong in supposing on this account that the self does not exist as a substantive unit. And much the same holds true of the psychology of James: To suggest that man is identical with his conscious states is to fail to explain the fact that it is in and through these states of consciousness that we are indeed conscious of *ourselves,* whatever we might analytically mean by the use of that term.[2]

What I am suggesting here therefore is that *a truly radical empiricism must take into account the reality of the experience that we have of ourselves as ourselves and as the dynamic centers of our activity.* At this point, however, we are immediately confronted with the problem: What or who is the "self"? I shall make no attempt at this point to conduct a long phenomenological inquiry into the self, but enough should be said to indicate that the principle of continuity in man is no mere psychological principle, but an ontological one. Further, it is erroneous to suppose, by the limitations of the method of pragmatism, that we have no experience of the self as an ontological center of our activities when as a matter of fact we do. Thus it is of *myself* that I am aware in all of my activities, so that I can rightly say that it is *I* who writes, eats, plays ball, goes to sleep at night, and so on. Consciousness, in other words, authentically reveals a real self that ontologically, and not merely psychologically, "lies beneath" our conscious states and it is a truncated form of empiricism that fails to recognize this essential point.

We have just seen that James through the limitations of his method failed to account for the deeper self that lies beneath our activities. One further point of criticism is in order. The pragmatism of James prevented him as well from

2. From the time I first began philosophy in the early '40's to the present I have yet to find a better discussion of the various problems and positions taken with respect to the substantiality of the human person than in a book that is long since out of print. The book in question is: Michael Maher's **Psychology** (New York: Longmans, Green, and Co., 1915, 8th ed.), see especially Chapter XXII, "False Theories of The Ego," pp. 474-492. In this chapter the author discusses Kant, Hume, Mill and James.

understanding that man is not only psychologically, but *ontologically* orientated to the values of his experience. I do not, of course, wish to indulge in any caricature of the pragmatism of James on the grounds that in a moment of enthusiasm he was carried away by the "cash value" of our ideas. Yet the truth of the matter is this: James in his exaggerated emphasis on the *will*-to-believe had lost sight of the ontological reference of our ideas. Let us take as a prime example his defense of the idea of God. According to James, God exists *if* my belief in God makes a practical difference in my life. Noble as the thought may be, the big question that remains is this: Does God really exist or not? From the point of view of a truly radical empiricism it would make all the difference in the world whether the object of my belief were something real or whether it were no more than a projection of my subconscious.

From a yet more positive point of view what I am trying to suggest is this: A truly radical empiricism is one which takes into account our ultimate concern with the question as to whether the values of our experience do or do not have a real basis in the outside world. There would be no point, for example, in my attempting to argue that Hitler did wrong in executing six million Jews unless I were not only convinced of it myself, but convinced as well that what he did *was* wrong according to an objective standard of morality —by which other persons could make the same kind of judgment as myself.

Pseudo and Authentic Empiricism

This much for the empiricism of James. Although I am in profound sympathy with the motivations that underlie it, I feel that James had failed in the final analysis to carry out the project he had so nobly begun. As for my own understanding, then, of a radical empiricism, let me make it clear first of all that it is characterized positively by its essential openness to any level of reality that lies outside the domain of the superficial level of the contents of our immediate experience. In other words, empiricism as I speak of it here cannot be the narrow empiricism which limits itself to the use of scientific method alone, but one which is open to all levels of reality whether they be artistic, scientific, philosophical, or religious. Empiricism of this sort—a truly radical empiricism—is based on the idea of the analogical character of experience, recognizing as it does the fact that there are many different levels and types of experience no one of which is simplistically or by any other means reducible to the other.

No doubt the greatest single prejudice of our time is the presupposition that experience—of whatever sort—must, in order to be valid, conform itself on a priori grounds to some single method of knowing—usually of a scientific kind. No presupposition, however, could be farther from the truth insofar as experience—in the full amplitude of its many-sided character—is pluralistic in nature and has a wide variety of dimensions that cannot be rigidly contained within any single method of interpreting it.

Let us be yet more explicit. One of the greatest single dangers in philosophy is the tendency (in whatever direction it may manifest itself) toward *reductionism*. Naturally enough, the philosopher has a pre-disposition to know how any given set of phenomena is contained in the categories with which he wishes to interpret those phenomena. Yet the point that is crucial is this: Should not the categories of the philosopher be themselves the very outcome of the contents of experience, and not the other way around? Certainly creativity has its limits, and it is a false creativity which makes the facts adjust to the theory and not the theory to the facts.

Back, then, to the meaning of a radical empiricism. A radical empiricism is *not* an empiricism that shuts itself off from the realm of supersensible existence. But to the contrary, it is essentially open to all levels of experience—the subconscious, the conscious and the rational, and most especially to the supra-conscious—this latter being a level of experience that totally transcends the contents of our immediate conscious and rational experience. Let me make my point clear. Freud was pre-eminently right when he fought as a pioneer in psychology for the unique and distinctive character of psychic experience as such. Contrary to many of his contemporaries he refused to *reduce* or explain away the levels of psychic experience in terms of physiological and biological categories. This much to the credit of Freud.

Yet much to the embarrassment of the Freudian technique, it must here be pointed out—and in unequivocal terms —that Freud himself had fallen into another kind of reductionism which he had already, in principle, condemned in his adversaries.

The reductionism in the Freudian method lay in a persistent attempt to construe the transcendent, ontological object of experience in terms of psychological categories alone. To Freud, for example, there is no *possibility* that God as a real entity exists and this for the "reason" that God is presupposed by Freud to be a projection of the father image in a manner that in no way conforms to a reality outside of itself. The central technique of Freud—in the realm of the supraconscious—was to drain psychological experience of any legitimate claim it might have to a real ontological content.

Not to become sidetracked by examples, I wish to reassert here that a truly radical empiricism—far from being opposed to the possibility of an ontological reality that lies outside our immediate experience—is essentially open to this or any other type of reality which is in some way related to the many different levels of experience.

Practical Considerations

If all of this seems abstract to the reader, let it be pointed out that empiricism, as we have known it in the last few hundred years in philosophy, has been too narrow, atomistic, and *a priori* in its methods to prove in any way satisfactory to the fullness of reality as we actually encounter it in our everyday lives. The need exists therefore—within the framework of an integral realism—for an enlarged empiricism that fully preserves the uniqueness of every aspect of human experience, *most of all those aspects of it that point the way toward a meaningful and objectively grounded transcendence.*

In favor, then, of the inherently analogical contents of experience I would suggest in outline form that there exist a variety of levels of experience, such as the following: The level of sense, the level of the subconscious, the level of the rational conscious (as including the level of scientific discourse), and finally the level of the suprarational (as including the many varieties of religious and mystical experiences). Only the narrowest type of empiricism would begin on the first two or three levels of experience while denying that any other level exists. In point of fact, it is this other level, which points to the supra-rational and supra-temporal needs of man, that should provide for man a subject of maximal interest, but whether it does or not, each level of experience should be carefully examined on its own terms and in its own right.

Permit me, then, at this point to digress. One of the greatest prejudices of the modern mind is the presupposition that the ultimate test of *all* experience is the primary level of sense. In other words, for most persons, sensible evidence and sensible evidence alone—conceived in the narrowest sense of the term—is the one and only valid criterion for the validity of any other type of experience. If, in the manner of Hume, an idea—of whatever sort—cannot be reduced to an image or impression of sense, then it has no more status than a chimera.

The great weakness, as I see it, in modern society is that men have by and large closed their eyes to the higher realms of the more deeply human and personal elements of experience and reduced these realms to the level of psychological categories as such. Psychologism—the great modern error initiated by the modern devaluation of the objective character of knowledge—is the doctrine that anything not verifiable by the immediate data of sense experience—is either a "projection" of the subconscious or a figment of the creative imagination.

One of the immediate corollaries of such a doctrine is this: The realm of the higher emotions, as including the realm of aesthetic and religious experience, is completely drained of any objective content of its own. On such an interpretation as this, there is no room for *understanding* ("intellectus vitae") as we spoke of it in an earlier chapter, but only for *knowledge* in the narrow, scientific sense of the term. Patriotism, for example, would be interpreted in this view as a noble sentiment, but not as something which—in terms of real values that affect men's lives—is *objectively* speaking, good in itself. Too, on such a psychologistical interpretation as this, art is an expression of the creative *emotions* of the artist, but in a way that is totally divorced from any inherent relation to reality itself. Finally, religion (in this same pragmatic and psychologistic mode of interpretation) is a remarkable human invention—designed, as in Dewey's philosophy, to relieve the "quest for certainty" or, as in Marx's to stifle the proletariat,—but it has no objective basis in fact on the grounds that any object of religious belief is no more than a projection of the subconscious mind as such.

Here, then, lies the ineradicable weakness of the empiricisms we have known in the last few hundred years. None of them—and this includes too the "radical" empiricism of James—does full justice to the inherently analogical character of experience. What is more, there is no form of radical empiricism in existence today that sufficiently grounds itself in the relationship between experience as a subjective affair and the ontological dimension of the reality to which it relates.

Conclusion

The role of philosophy is not to tell men what they *should* experience if they have no experience of a given object at all. Nor is it, for that matter, the role of philosophy to defend the objective character of every imaginable type of experience. Men, after all, do suffer from illusions, and the philosopher, far from consolidating these illusions, should do whatever he can to unmask them whether they issue from Francis Bacon's "idols of the cave" or the "idols of the market place" or any other source. More funda-

118

mentally, however, it is the role of the philosopher to interpret—in an open and sympathetic manner—all different
types of experience so that no one type of experience is
reduced to the categories of any other. Least of all should
the philosopher find himself guilty of interpreting the
whole of experience in terms of a few rigid categories that
are the inventions of his own mind.

One of the reasons, therefore, why philosophy as we
know it today has fallen into a moribund state is its radical
failure to take a more liberal view of experience of the sort
that characterizes the spirit and motivation of a William
James. Even to this day philosophy has become "bogged
down," or, if you choose, "hung up" by the narrow, atomistic
empiricism of Locke, Hume and Mill. As I have pointed out
earlier, the problem with philosophers—with their exaggerated concern to imitate the methods of science—is that of
a loss of nerve that has led to a myopic distortion of the true
meaning of human experience on all of its many levels. After
all, it takes more than a measure of intellectual courage to
project hypotheses that carry one beyond the range of
scientific method as such. What I am saying, of course,
would be considered rank heresy by Dewey in view of his
own precommitment to the "supremacy of method" along
scientific lines. Yet the point of this chapter is to show that
science and the methods of science are no ultimate paradigm
(as Dewey had wrongly imagined them to be) for each
and every type of experience. By a strange paradox therefore it has turned out that Dewey's metaphysics of experience
is no metaphysics at all, not even indeed a phenomenology
of experience, but an attempt to reduce it to one single
method, to a uniform mold. The intent of this chapter has
been to show that any such attempt is not only futile but

contrary to the spirit of what a true empiricism should be—open to any and all levels of experience, artistic, scientific, philosophical, and religious. In the chapter that follows I want to show that such a radical empiricism is not only compatible with a philosophy of self-transcendence, but that it opens the door to a yet higher realm of values that the earlier forms of empiricism have denied.

8

THE PRIMACY OF SELF-TRANSCEN-DENCE

Introductory Remark

One of the great objectives of philosophy as therapy, especially as social therapy, is to help man to understand himself. In the first place, when I speak of "modern man" I am not using an empty abstraction. As I have pointed out earlier, men today are influenced, however subconsciously so, by all the antecedents of the culture in which they live, and these influences have shaped what we have called the "modern mind." By "modern mind" I mean pre-eminently—in the context of Western culture—a mind that has become enclosed and entwined for the last four hundred years in the categories of its own subjective states. Let us explore further how the therapy of self-transcendence can counteract the subjectivism of our times.

The All-Pervasive Character of Subjectivism

Modern philosophy began with Descartes in the subjectivism of the formula *Cogito ergo sum* (I think therefore I am). Strangely enough, Hume's own brand of empiricism, though opposed to the rationalism of Descartes, served only to re-emphasize the subjectivism of that tradition. This is to say that Hume, equally as much as Descartes, had imprisoned the human psyche within the consciousness of its own introspective states. Kant, though critical of Hume, reinforced the tendency toward subjectivism through his own peculiar doctrine of *a priori* forms. But this was not all, inasmuch as the tendency toward subjectivism received new life and fresh impetus with the advent of psychology as we know it today. Though the development of psychology marked a positive step toward knowing the subconscious motivations of human behavior, it also opened the door to a new kind of reductionism. My own attitude toward psychology is, of course, a positive one, and I fully appreciate the advance that was made—especially through Freud and Jung—toward understanding the subconscious motivations of human behavior. However, the discovery of the unconscious was marked, not by a rejection of the previously established subjective theories of knowing, but by a further attempt—in a different direction—to reduce all knowing to the level of the psychological states of mind. In a word, psychology began and continued, as we observed in our last chapter, with an attempt to reduce the ontological—the order of being—to the categories of the subjective as such. What with all of its emphasis on the necessity of establishing a contact between mind and reality, the theory of Freud and others tended to *reduce* reality—especially its upper realms—to the level of subconscious mind. In a word, psychology had become so intoxicated with its discovery of the depths of our subconscious states that it was led to interpret everything through these states alone.

Such, then, is the plight of the modern mind that—caught up in centuries of conditioning to subjectivism in one or another of its forms, whether rationalistic or "empirical"—

it has lost sight on almost all sides of its own capacity for transcendence. No doubt the reader will justifiably object to my statement on the grounds that in the area of science the modern mind *has* transcended itself; and this I readily concede. However, in any other realm than that defined by the method of science—*especially in the realm of values*—modern man has lost confidence in his ability simply to *know*. As I have elsewhere explained, the natural realism of the human mind has been blocked off by all the currents of scepticism that have invaded it for the past four hundred years.

What is important to know at this point is the necessity of recognizing the situation as it actually is. If modern man is caught up in the throes of subjectivism particularly in the area of religious truth, and he is led to believe that this is a natural condition of the human intelligence—when in point of fact it is not—then there is very little room for hope. This is to say that the work of philosophy as therapy cannot possibly be exercised in any effective way until and unless the disease is recognized for what it is—*as* a disease and not as a condition of health. As in medical affairs, most often the patient himself is the last to admit that he is really sick when it is painfully obvious to everyone else that he is.

The situation, however, is not as hopeless as it seems, and to be aware of this we need only direct our attention to the obvious yet mysterious fact that there exists a radical tendency within human nature, however deeply buried it may be under the layers of modern subjectivism, toward self-transcendence. Particularly in the American temperament—so it seems to the prejudiced view of this author—is there a mighty reserve of good sense that cannot ultimately be repressed by the contrary influences that have prevailed for so long a time.

Knowledge as Self-Transcendence

Many persons are frightened or at least bewildered by the word "transcendence." To them the "transcendent" means (by its very definition) something highly mysterious that lies totally outside the range of experience. No little surprise, then, to such persons, that knowledge itself—even the simplest and most obvious forms of it like the knowledge I have of my dog—is a form of self-transcendence. To see how and why this is so, consider what a totally distorted view it is to regard knowledge as nothing more than the confinement of the self to its own subjective states. True enough, this is the great lie of all the major epistemologies of the last few hundred years. But the fact that this lie was sustained—will it or not—by the great philosophical geniuses of modern times in no way attenuates its character as a lie. Rightly, then, do the phenomenologists insist—from Husserl on—that the most basic feature of human knowing is its other-directedness. Human knowing is directed toward an object outside of and distinct from itself or from the one who happens to know. To say that I am conscious at all is to imply that I am conscious in some way of somebody or something—real or imaginary, actual or possible. Beyond any shadow of doubt therefore, knowledge of whatever sort implies of its very essence a kind of self-transcendence by which the knower somehow "identifies" with the object that lies (ordinarily) outside of, and is distinct from, himself as knower.

Self-Transcendence and Ultimate Concern

So much at this point for the question of self-transcendence as knowledge: quite simply the classical epistemolo-

124

gies have failed to rescue the individual from the barriers of his introspective states. From a yet larger viewpoint I am concerned with the problem of the meaning of self-transcendence as love. In this connection I ask the reader to recall one of the basic problems of this book, which is to examine why modern man has become a problem to himself.

In a previous chapter we have seen that man—all protestations to the contrary—is a metaphysical being who, will it or not, is inclined by nature to reach for a good, some ultimate good, outside of himself. The unhappy condition of modern man, however, is his persistent attempt, in view of his slavish dependence upon finite goods as such, to deny —whether in practice or in theory—that such is the case. Modern man has chosen instead to regard himself only as a biological organism, as a being who has no ultimate concern other than catering to the needs of a purely conventional wisdom.

The leading contention of this book, though, is to submit that all of the problems of modern man originate in this central error—of man's refusal to admit that he is all that he is, in the totality of his physical, cultural, and above all, his spiritual, being. In a word, every psychological conflict and hence the neuroses that symptomize these conflicts, is a manifestation of the refusal to admit that man is by definition a person who in the depths of his nature is a creature of ultimate concern. But let the matter rest at that, as I want to explore more deeply both the need and the nature of self-transcendence as love.

Historical Considerations

Earlier in this volume I spoke of the various types of

125

voluntarisms that have preempted the philosophical scene over the last one hundred years. I have spoken of Schopenhauer's insistence on the primacy of the will-to-live, of Nietzsche's avowal of the will-to-power, of James' will-to-believe, and of the Freudian will-to-pleasure, and in more recent times, of Frankl's more wholesome insistence on the will-to-meaning. I should be the last, of course, to deny that man does have the will to live, to have power, to believe, and all the rest; yet we should never ignore the fact that man is more than a biological unit, and for this reason it is wrong to place an exaggerated emphasis on such factors as the will to live, and so on. Everything alive has the will to live and tends as far as possible to preserve itself in being, but this is hardly a unique and all-pervasive character of the human psyche in the sense of having an absolute priority over every other aspect of human behavior. Does not man ask himself, for example, *why* he should go on living, what the meaning of life is, and the like? As for the will-to-power, Nietzsche was right, of course, even as Kierkegaard earlier, in conducting a radical criticism of the defects of a declining Christian culture such as he experienced it in his time. Yet the doctrine of the "overman," triumphing over the shattered ruins of those unfortunate creatures who lost out in the battle of life, is hardly a satisfactory *modus vivendi* for those who aspire to some nobler goal than that of absolute power. In fact, Nietzsche's own counterpart of Darwin's survival of the fittest was hardly an advance over the thesis maintained by Hobbes long ago, that the original state of mankind was one of universal war of all against all (*bellum omnium contra omnes*).

As for the Jamesian doctrine of the will-to-believe, it is certainly true, as James contends, that man has a right to believe, and that in many cases it is better to believe than to let life pass on by. Yet belief for James seems to be too much of an emergency affair, a sort of last resort where no certain knowledge is attainable. Most especially, the inherent weakness of the Jamesian doctrine of the will-to-believe is shortsightedness with respect to the *object* of belief. Whether belief is meaningful or not should depend, so it seems to me, not on the question of whether one has a *right* to believe, but on the question of whether one *is* right in what he believes. The question, in other words, of the object of belief should be established on other than purely pragmatic grounds.

In any case, the will-to-believe is too much of an exclusively psychological affair as James made it out to be, but let the matter ride at that. It is certain in any event that James, penetrating psychologist that he was, could hardly agree with Freud in the latter's universal insistence on the will-to-pleasure. The pleasure motive, important and fundamental as it is as a source of human motivation and behavior, can hardly be interpreted legitimately as the essential spark of existence. In fact, one can become satiated with pleasure to the point of disgust, and realize at that point that he has reached a dead-end street. It is therefore by some further motive than pleasure that quite often marks the return from hedonism to a more meaningful way of life.

As I see it, the closest anyone has come in recent years to the very center of human existence is the discovery made by Viktor Frankl that men can put up with an immense amount of pain, misery, and suffering, if by some means they can be restored to a sense of hope and to an understanding of the meaning of their lives both for others and for themselves. To me it is a remarkable thing that this fundamental truth, as the will-to-meaning, was discovered *empirically* (by a *radical* empiricism, I would insist) by a psychologist in a Nazi concentration camp. But however great the discovery was in itself, Frankl's own exploration of it was limited for the most part to the methods of psychology alone.

Without wishing, therefore, to detract either from the truth or the originality of Frankl's discovery, I want to emphasize here that there is a need for a yet deeper philosophical analysis of what lies beyond the will-to-meaning in terms of what I have called self-transcendence through love.

Levels of Self-Transcendence

As a prolegomenon to the further discussion of the meaning of self-transcendence, let me say first of all that the soul of modern man—and I use this word without apologies to Hume or anyone else—needs above all to be nursed back to a state of health; and by "health" I mean the kind of health that results from a wholesome interplay —in realistic and ecological terms—between man and his external environment. Mistake not my words as I am not a Deweyan environmentalist, least of all of the behaviorist variety. What I am stressing here rather is man's *fundamental need for a redeeming contact,* first on the level of sense, and then on the level of his whole being—intellect, emotion (especially the higher emotions, as I shall speak of them later), and will. The encounter should not be with man's own states of mind, but with *being,* as it is given to him in the world outside of himself. It is with a sense of deep urgency that I use the term "being" as it is a flight from reality —engendered by an endless variety of subjectivisms—that has catapulted modern man into a state of atrophy, impotence, and ill-psychological health. Man, in short, is not a solitary creature who can for long isolate himself from his environment in the hopes of regaining in this state of isolation, of self-imposed solitary confinement, a consciousness of that which is ultimately real.

Here, then, lies the central paradox of modern man: knowing in the depths of his subconscious that "no man is an island" and what is yet more important, that no man can with impunity ignore metaphysical truths (especially those of ultimate concern), he has nonetheless chosen to live as if these truths had no significance—immanent or transcendent —for his personal life. In short, modern man has traded off his soul for what I have come to regard as the "problems of the executive class"—the sort of problems that pertain to one's material life as such and the conditions of expanding it beyond any reason or significance. While the contrived needs of the ego in such a materialist culture are overfed to the point of disgust, the natural needs of the soul, needs for love, beauty and truth, are kept in abeyance for the better part, if not for the totality, of one's life.[1]

But let us proceed at this point to the real meaning of transcendence. What does it mean for a person to transcend himself? Certainly not that one should jump out of his skin: transcendence does not in any case mean the abandonment or loss of one's own personality. To the very contrary, the

---

1. Here I am trying to show the element of profound stupidity that is involved in the modern identification of happiness with the affluence of modern life. Modern man, thinking to avoid the necessary confrontation with the self, has set up for himself the many escape hatches which affluence can provide in the hope of avoiding the deeper issues of life itself. The basic crisis, then, that emerges from this escape mentality is one of self-identity, the failure of man to identify with the ultimate reality of his **real** self, which is to say, of his own fundamental nature as man.

real meaning of the person as an inner dynamic source of activity can be effected only by a living contact with the world outside of oneself. Man would be no better off than a carrot or a plum if he were restricted to the "environment" only of himself.

The question that faces us, then, is this: what can we know about the life of man as man, insofar as it is *different* from that of any living thing inferior to himself? To answer this question, consider the difference between a dead duck and one that is alive and kicking: a dead duck cannot move except through an outside source, as for example, when its feathers are moved by the wind. If, however, a thing is alive, it contains within itself its own principle of self-motion in proportion to the degree of its inner life.

Plants, for example, have life, but only minimally so, since they can do no more than take nourishment, grow, and generate their own kind. Animals, of course, are more perfect than plants because they do have the power of transcendence through knowledge. By a natural instinct they propel themselves to the known sensible goods of their environment. What differentiates man from anything else, however, is his power to compare in his own mind the various types of ends he might wish to pursue. Man, in other words, is not "tied down" to one thing or compulsively driven by natural instinct alone. Most important of all, he has the capacity to judge, reason, and reflect as to alternative courses of action, or under certain conditions he may choose not to act at all.

Let us dwell on this point. Man's remarkable capacity for transcendence over the problems of his environment is engendered by his natural ability to use both his intelligence and his free will. Knowing through his intelligence that there *are* different possibilities of action he is free, in a way

The Primacy of Self-Transcendence

that animals are not, to *choose* what he considers to be good and in addition to this, he is free as to the choice of means. What I want to emphasize here is the absolute uniqueness of freedom insofar as it takes its root in the reflective intelligence of man. Further, man's natural freedom, such as it exists, means relative transcendence over the "tyranny" of the environment.

Unfortunately, the pragmatism of Dewey placed a one-sided emphasis on this kind of transcendence. The purpose of knowledge in Dewey's philosophy is to modify the conditions of environment to the manipulation of man's biological needs. But is it right to suppose that the biological needs of man—however broadly we interpret them—are primary, as if man were an end unto himself? To answer this question, consider that man is capable of a kind of transcendence that goes far beyond either a mere knowledge or control of his environment. Man also has the capacity of transcendence through love.[2]

Love, of course, is always in some sense based on knowledge, even though in many cases it is said to be "blind." But the difference between knowledge and love is this: to know something is to adjust the condition of the object to the needs of the knower as such. Every knower, so to speak,

---

2. This means that within the depths of his soul man experiences a hidden yearning for transcendence, for the transcendence of an outgoing love that can lead to personal development and a full human life. But instead of feeding this appetite with the goods that it necessarily craves, man has created for himself an "ersatz" appetite for the goods of a material culture that can only in the end lead him down the road of despair. In the end he experiences a kind of spiritual paralysis, a loss of freedom, that forces him to cry out for release. The real challenge, then, to philosophy today is to show modern man, in a renewed perspective, the way in which he can recover his sense of dignity and nobility from the multitudinous distractions and distortions of modern life.

131

proportions the object to his own needs, "cuts it down" to his own size. The situation is reversed, however, in the case of transcendence through love: in loving something, preferably some*one*, we want to unite ourselves *really*—not merely intentionally—with the "object" of our love, the point being that love is an outgoing motion that refuses to rest until it has met its term.

If, for example, a young man is in love with a girl, it is no ultimate satisfaction for him to be possessed of her photograph or only to dream of her. None of these things is an adequate substitute for the presence of the person herself. Yet this is not all. Love seeks its union through activity, the sort of activity by which the lover adjusts himself to the desires of his beloved. In this sense love always involves a displacement—a sense of personal discomfort—that knowledge by itself does not. In knowing something we do not have to change our lives for that which we know; in loving something, we must. As St. Augustine (354-430) said long ago, "*Amor meus, pondus meum*" ("My love is my weight"). Further, love has a way of stirring us up to do things—to dance, to cook, to get dressed for dinner—things we might never do without love. All of this because in a manner of speaking the lover no longer has a life of his own: he lives for the one he loves. To love someone, then, is to act for the good of the person that one loves.

Transcendence as Therapy: Royce and the Beloved Community

Subjectivism is a two-pronged affair: as a denial of the transcendence of knowledge it leads to scepticism and as a denial of love in the affective order it leads to the syndrome of the isolated self. Such, then, is the condition of modern society that those who share in the bitter fruits of its impersonal modes of existence—almost of necessity—lead lives that are shut off from vital communion with their fellow human beings.

The ultimate reason therefore why modern man has become a problem to himself is that the conditions of modern life have made it difficult—if not impossible under certain circumstances—for him to achieve the degree of self-transcendence that he so radically and deeply needs as a human being. Most people are by nature inclined to be generous, but if nobody wants them or needs them, they tend to become too shy to exert the courage that is necessary to get outside of themselves. They begin instead, to develop all sorts of symptoms—many of them psychosomatic in character—that carry them down the path of an introverted self-concern which leads from one neurosis to another.

One of the greatest human needs, therefore, is for man to develop a sense of community. But a *sense* of community is all but impossible unless one actually *lives* in community. It is in and through the vital contacts one establishes in community life that one grows and develops as a person.

This, at any rate, is part of the meaning of self-transcendence. But there is more to it than that. Man must not only live *in* community, but he must also perform in community those tasks that are most properly suited to those talents and abilities that are uniquely his own. What is more, it is highly important that those living in community give proper recognition to every person for the tasks he performs—lest anyone be reduced to the level of "object" or function rather than be recognized for what he is as a person.

At this point I should like to stress the profound element of truth that characterizes the thought of the great American idealist, Josiah Royce (1855-1916). Personally, I find Royce's notion of "The Absolute," together with the highly contrived elements of his metaphysical system, equally as unpalatable as did James and Peirce. Yet it is the social thought of Royce that makes him the great philosopher that he is, and most especially that element of it which stresses the ideal of the "beloved community."[3]

More than any single American philosopher, Royce made it clear that man has a radical, not merely an incidental, need to live in community with his fellow-man. More profoundly, however, Royce has also shown that all men living in community have an obligation to serve a "cause" higher than themselves. Husband and wife serve the "cause" of their marriage insofar as the love they have for each other is something greater, something if you will, that transcends their individual and isolated selves; civil workers serve the "cause" of justice, again, in a way that transcends the interests of the individual as such. Ultimately, all men in the view of Royce are destined to live in a world community in which ideally there is a proper balance between the rights of the individual as such and the growth of the community one serves.

So much for Royce. I now want to gather up some of the insights of the last few pages. Self-transcendence as love means many things. It means *living* in community, but also *acting for the good of that community.* It also means *sharing*

3. See especially Josiah Royce's, **The Problems of Christianity** (New York: The Macmillan Co, 1913), Vol. II, Lectures 9 and 10 on the nature of the community. These same essays are reproduced in M. Fisch's **Classic American Philosophers** (New York: Appleton-Century-Crofts, Inc., 1951), pp. 200-212. For Royce's classic set of lectures on modern philosophy see his work, **The Spirit of Modern Philosophy** (New York: W. W. Norton and Co., Inc., 1967), a paperback reprint of the original.

in the goods in which the community shares and *receiving* the measure of recognition, love, and affection that is proper to anyone who has thus devoted himself to a "cause." It has been my contention all along that much of the sickness of the modern world is the result of this lack of sharing. As Marcel (under the influence, incidentally, of Royce) has rightly pointed out, for man to exist is for him to *co-exist* with others.

Further Horizons

Beyond the idea of self-transcendence as love in community there are various other aspects of it that we shall only hint at before we close this chapter. For one thing, when I speak of the *primacy* of transcendence I am not stating a proposition that goes beyond the bounds of a radical empiricism. The empiricisms of the past have been too narrow and confining to do justice to this idea, whereas a truly radical empiricism is open to *all* of the higher values of life.

More important, however, than anything we have said in this chapter is this yet further and more profound aspect of the meaning of self-transcendence: there is a certain dynamism within every human being by which in some way or another he seeks to improve his lot. Some persons, in the fashion of empire builders for example, seek to transcend themselves by way of acquisition and control. Their prototype is Alexander the Great, who wept because he thought that there were no further worlds to conquer. But this is a false and mistaken notion of transcendence, reminiscent of the failure to make the distinction made by Marcel, between "being" and "having." To add to one's possessions, or power, or control is to follow the path of a horizontal transcendence over the environment that in no way adds to the enrichment of the person himself.

Self-transcendence, therefore, if it is to be truly authentic must be a transcendence that takes place in the depths and not on the surface of things. What it implies most of all is a steady and persistent desire to reach up to the realization of values that are higher than the "self." So conceived, self-transcendence is an ultimate source of motivation that lies within the depths of the psyche for liberation through the action of love. Just as matter, by a dynamic evolutionary process, constantly reaches up to the possession of yet higher forms, so does the human psyche (once properly oriented) tend to transform itself, not by a narrow concentration on the self, but by a total dedication to something or someone higher than the self.

A Postscript on the Nature of Values

The whole meaning of self-transcendence as I have tried to develop it in this chapter would be lost if it were imagined that the realm of values were a purely subjective realm. Admittedly, there are no values unless there is an evaluating subject, but this is not to say that man purely and simply creates the realm of values without some reference to their factual basis in experience. Thus it is false to imagine that the goodness of things is in every instance derivative from the values we attach to them. This may be so in the case of artifacts like money or rare gems. But more fundamentally, the goodness of some things and actions is itself the reason why we evaluate them as we do. For example, the "value" of the person is not something that derives from custom or caprice. There is something in the reality of the person as an "ontological unit" that makes him more valuable than money or any type of exchangeable goods, and this we consider to be a fact, not a theory.

What is important to know therefore is that self-transcendence cannot take place until and unless there is at least an implicit realization of the objective foundations of some of the values of our experience. Further, it is important for philosophers to know—especially life-philosophers—that the dichotomy between "values" and "facts" is not as rigid as many of them imagine it to be. As a matter of fact, values are themselves a certain kind of fact, and they are objectively related to the real world in which we live and have our being.

Conclusion

The reason modern man has suffered from a sickness-unto-death is his persistent refusal to act on the basis of what in point of fact he is—a metaphysical being. Will it or not, man is a creature of ultimate concern, and this ultimate concern cannot be successfully achieved within the narrow confines of the self. Hence the need—on many different levels—for self-transcendence. Ultimately, it is not simply the will-to-live, the will-to-power, the will-to-pleasure, or what have you, that supplies the deepest motivation for human behavior, but the will-to-self-transcendence. Once this fact is known, it is important from that point on to distinguish the forms of inauthentic self-transcendence from those that are not. In general, self-transcendence on its highest level is but another name for love.

9

INCARNA-
TIONAL
PHILOSOPHY:
WHAT IS IT?

*Introductory
Remarks*

ALL APPEARANCES
to the contrary, philosophy is a thing of human concern.
Beginning especially with Socrates, philosophy became an
endeavor to look for some element of unity and meaning, not
only in nature, but in man himself. To our own day this is
largely what philosophy is or should be about, namely, to
discover not merely the logical meaning of concepts, but the
real meaning of human life. As integral realism, a true and
authentic philosophy should reconcile and *integrate* the legitimate demands both of a radical empiricism and the need,
as we have spoken of it in our previous chapter, for transcendence. From a modern point of view the great problem
of philosophy is not so much that of the "one and the many"
as conceived in purely abstract and metaphysical terms, as
it is the problem of immanence and transcendence conceived
in meta-psychological terms with reference to the "problem
of man."

Although philosophy takes its roots in the past, it must
also cope with the problem of man in his present milieu.
Philosophers, of course, are right in supposing that the evolution of philosophy should parallel the growth and development of art, literature, and science. They are wrong, however, if they imagine that the continued growth of philoso-

Incarnational Philosophy: What Is It?

phy is dependent on a slavish imitation of the methods of science. As we have previously noted, philosophy has a method and aim peculiar to itself, and the life of philosophy depends on the strength of this conviction. But this is not all. If philosophy is to take a new push forward, it must at this point make a clean break with the inhibiting scepticisms of the past. Philosophy must sink its roots deep in the inner life of man and respond not to the contrived needs of a decadent philosophical tradition, but to the authentic needs of the human spirit. It must, in a word, achieve a new type of synthesis between a true radical empiricism, as set forth in Chapter Seven, and a total wisdom that bases itself on the ultimate realities of life.

Why "Incarnational"?

The aim of this chapter is to develop further the idea of what an integral realism should be in an attempt not only to preserve, but to augment the value of the human intelligence in the life of man. I shall do this against the background of the central thesis of this book—that true philosophy has a liberating influence in the life of the human spirit that few other disciplines possess, and that, indeed, philosophy, equally as much and even more so than psychology, is equipped to provide modern man with a therapy of its own.

It is a mistake, of course, to imagine that a therapy is also a panacea, a sort of gimmick to cure all human ills. Philosophy makes no such claim, nor do I mean to propose, for that matter, that any single philosophy is or can be a completely rounded-off product, like a "package deal" that one accepts or rejects on a "take it or leave it" basis. To the very contrary, philosophy, like any other achievement of the human spirit, is something that grows and develops with the growth and development of the human spirit itself. It is something organic and evolutionary, admitting as it does of constant development and improvement, and from time to time, of the need for a total reconstruction of the sort that helps it to achieve a new plateau.

But back to the point at hand. We have already seen, in spite of many attempts to deny the fact, that man is a metaphysical being. As such he is endowed, or better, "possessed" with a certain restlessness of the spirit, an "existential neurosis," which demands that sooner or later he face up to the problems of ultimate concern. One cannot without impunity go through life ignoring questions which go to the very heart of our existence while giving full scope and exclusive attention to matters of trivial concern. In the long run it makes little difference which brand of toothpaste a person uses, the kind of car he drives, or clothes that he wears; but it does make a difference whether or not he can discover some kind of purpose. Accordingly, a true philosophy is one that recognizes not only the immediacies of experience, but also those very problems of ultimate concern. It must be realistic, goal-directed, empirical, and transcendent. Beyond all this, however, it must also strive to become "incarnational" in a sense we shall presently explain.

From the time of its classical splendor, philosophy, especially under the aegis of Plato, had subjected itself to the dualism of "two worlds"—the world of the suprasensible and what comprised for Plato the shadowy world of sensible things which were no more than sharings in the yet higher realms of "ideas" or "forms." It is against the dualism of Plato that I propose the idea, in modern terms, of an incarnational philosophy which recognizes in man the *totality* of his human nature. In a sense never sufficiently explored by Plato, appearances *do* manifest the reality that lies underneath, and it is unequivocally true that the "appearances" of flesh and blood and bones do manifest the real character of man. The human body, in other words, is no mere epiphenomenon of spirit, but in a very profound sense, it is the living reality of the man himself. To posit, as Plato did, a dualism between "body" and "soul," or, as Descartes did, between "body" and "mind," is to lose sight of the fundamental fact that man is an integral unit that is in no way reducible either to a disembodied spirit or a corpse.

The point at issue here, in view of the anthropocentric character of an integral realism, is the necessity of an "incarnational" approach to the problem of man. In view of my previous references to the needs of the "soul" and the "spirit," the reader may possibly accuse me of being inconsistent on this point. How, he might ask, can you speak of an "incarnational" philosophy, while all along you have given the impression that the human self is ultimately identified with the soul?

If I have given that impression I have misled my reader indeed, and if so, I must set the record straight. By the "soul" of man I do not mean a separately existing substance that is, as it were, housed in the "prison" of the body till the time of its effective release after death. I make no judgment here, of course, about the meaning of life after death as that is a separate question by itself.[1] What I am saying, however, is

1. In other words, although I believe in personal immortality on religious grounds, and hold this doctrine to be entirely reasonable in the light of philosophy, I do not propose in the text to present any of the proofs for personal immortality. Basically, these proofs are either moral or metaphysical. The metaphysical proofs argue on the basis of the kind of a being man is (as known through his activities) that the soul as a substantial principle, though not as a complete substance in itself,

that what I call "soul" is itself the living reality that gives the body its life—the reality that totally pervades that living thing which we call the "body" of man. Grasped in his essential unity man is neither "soul" nor "body" by itself. He is but a single, though complex, thing or substance that has a life peculiarly its own.

So much for a basic statement of the existential reality we call "man." Less basic perhaps but equally important for our consideration is the fact that man—as a creature of flesh, body, and bone—is indeed, as Dewey rightly proposes, a "biological unity" that is constantly in a process of development. Man is not a static entity, and it is entirely reasonable to suppose a human evolution that is integrally related to cosmic evolution at large. To what extent man is an outgrowth of his historical antecedents is not for us to say at this point. What I wish to assert, however, in agreement with the naturalists, is that there exists genetically a radical continuity between man and the rest of his environment. This radical immanence of man, however, is not so all-pervasive as to make it impossible for man to take a leap forward beyond any and all those forms of life that lie below the level of the human species as such.

Stated in simple terms, matter has a natural tendency to rise above its presently existing states; it is something dynamically oriented toward growth and constantly seeks

continues to exist on a personal basis after death. The moral proofs proceed to show the **need** for immortality on the basis of an adequate reward for one's good deeds while here on earth. As for the question of the "reunion of the body with the soul" (though this terminology is somewhat misleading), it is not possible for philosophy to prove that such a reunion takes place after death. However, it a matter of religious belief both among Christians and others besides that man after death will enjoy—at some future date—this state of reunion. This doctrine is traditionally known as that of the "resurrection" of the body.

142

to achieve in this process a degree of excellence or perfection that it lacked in its elementary forms. If, then, we apply this concept to the total reality of man we are obliged to say that this matter which is the reality of the human organism is the result of a long evolutionary process by which gradually and over many millions of years it evolved from certain lower forms to the present high level of its existence.

Lest it be thought that I am proposing an all-out naturalism with respect to the origin of man, let me state quite emphatically that man is more than his historical antecedents insofar as he incorporates within himself a principle of life that totally transcends the lower levels of material existence such as we find them in the life of plants and brutes. What is more, it is unreasonable to suppose, from a strictly philosophical point of view, that the evolutionary process, particularly with respect to man, is purely and simply the result of a set of blind forces that by some fortuitous combination of events led to the development of man as we know him today.

What I am trying to say therefore is that although man is a biological unity, he is also something more than that insofar as he, at least in some of his distinctive operations and activities, totally transcends the limitations of matter. This is to say that there exists within the totality of this being we call man, a spiritual principle of life that is itself transcendent over the laws of matter as such—namely, the reality of the human psyche. Man is psyche and organism in one, and it is the uniqueness of the human psyche, inexplicable in terms of the laws of matter alone, that gives a stamp of uniqueness to the living reality of man.

Earlier in this volume I spoke of the need for a "meta-psychology" in a sense that transcends the meaning of that term as used by analytic philosophers as an essential part of an integral realism in philosophy. My present endeavor is to explain in yet more precise terms that a true metapsychology—of the reality of man—is an integral approach *in depth* to the totality of human nature; and this is a concept insufficiently grasped either by the empiricisms or the rationalisms of the past few hundred years. Having prepared the stage therefore for a more enlarged understanding of an "incarnational" approach to the problem of man, we are now in a position to see the fundamental error of all past philosophies that have exaggerated either the purely biological aspects of human existence or those that we might call "spiritual." Man is, all in one, a spiritual organism who is capable, in the line of evolutionary change, of indefinite expansion and growth. Too, as we have repeatedly insisted, he is no mere captive of his psychological impulses, but a person of ultimate metaphysical concern.

Incarnationalism in Philosophy: Some of Its Practical Implications

Enough has been said to show what we mean by an incarnational approach to man. Such an approach regards man neither simplistically as a biological unit nor as a pure spirit. What is important at this stage of our study is an examination in depth of some of the practical implications of the viewpoint we have been trying to establish.

On the ethical and political plane Karl Marx was profoundly right in stressing as he did the relevancy of the economic factor in the process of social evolution, and to this extent we might even say that he too was an "incarnational" philosopher. What is lacking, however, in Marx, as in all of the naturalists of contemporary vintage, is an adequate understanding of the depths of the human psyche. The great point of confusion, not only in Marx, but in all of the evolutionary naturalisms of the past, is the failure to distinguish between a mentalistic philosophy and one that stresses in radically empirical terms the living dynamism of the human psyche. Rightly, in other words, did Marx and certain other life-philosophers of the last century direct their criticism against a mentalistic approach to man as though, by some contrived effort of the human imagination, man's life were the epistemological one of discovering how he could know "reality" in the first place. In spite of the finely spun arguments of George Berkeley's (1685-1753) *Three Dialogues Between Hylas and Philonus,* it is unequivocally true to say that man, through the transcendence of human knowledge, is directly and immediately in contact with the objects and persons of his experience.

This being said, however, it is false to reject, along with the mentalism of classical modern philosophy, the whole idea of man as psyche and spirit. To speak of man as spirit is not to posit in man a principle of life unrelated to the life of the body organism, but rather one which gives it its meaning. As some of the older philosophers used to say in a manner beyond their own realization of the truth: matter exists for the sake of "form"; and from a modern evolutionary viewpoint, the lower forms exist for the sake of the higher.

Let us paraphrase what we have said: the concept of man as spirit, far from being at odds with an incarnational approach to man, is one which views man in the higher as well as the lower aspects of his being, and for this very reason it is true to say that Marx and other contemporary materialists have, in spite of their best efforts, adopted a short-sighted view of the totality of human nature. The problem of human nature is the problem of reconciling the data that relate both to the established facts of human immanence *and* transcendence. Accordingly, to deny the transcendence of man is to refuse to meet the problem on its own terms, and to fall prey to a position that falls below the level of an *integral* realism.

But let us move on at this point in the positive direction of discovering the practical implications of incarnationalism in philosophy. One of the chief implications is this: philosophy in its deepest sense cannot and should not restrict itself to a purely "cerebral" approach to the problem of man. By this I do not mean to suggest, of course, that philosophy has no speculative value. Rather, to the extent that philosophy is a speculative wisdom it must according to the very etymology of the term take a long look at all that is discoverable in the reality of man. "Speculor" as a Latin verb means that I look at something in the sense not merely of a casual glance, but in the sense of penetrating observation and *understanding*.

The point then is this: a truly speculative approach to man must be as many-sided in its dimensions as is man himself in his being. It must view human nature not merely from one limited aspect (as did Marx from the economic point of view), but from the many varied aspects of human behavior.[2] The problem here is to develop an approach to man that gets beyond the structure of his being to the many different types of activities in which, for various reasons, he engages himself. An old scholastic axiom reads to the effect that operation or activity manifests being. Our concern here is to show that the multi-faceted activity (artistic, literary, religious, and so on) of human nature reveals not

---

2. For a good contemporary discussion of Marx's philosophy, see John Somerville's, **The Philosophy of Marxism, An Exposition** (New York: Random House, 1967). See also Louis Dupré's, **The Philosophical Foundations of Marxism** (New York: Harcourt, Brace, and World, Inc., 1966).

only phenomenologically but *really* (though in varying degrees), the depths of the being we call man.

Aristotle no doubt was right in suggesting that man is "rational," but a too exclusive emphasis on human rationality as such will lead us to imagine that man is a sort of logic machine. Accordingly, it is incumbent on anyone who is bent on an incarnational approach to man to discover in depth and at leisure those other aspects of human behavior that lead us to a yet deeper knowledge of the reality of man. For example, is it not true to say that man is also *homo faber* (man the worker), *homo ludens* (man the player and the dawdler), *homo sapiens* (man seeking wisdom), and the like? Most important of all perhaps is that dimension of human nature by which we come to understand man as one whose activities *as lover (homo amator,* if you will) give rise to the very meaning of his life. As we noted in our previous chapter, man is a being who constantly seeks to transcend himself, especially through love.

Incarnationalism and Inter-Personal Relationships

Much has been said in recent years concerning a need for a thorough understanding of "person." To this I say "amen" in view of the fact that the excessively analytical approach of philosophers to the problem of man has all but distorted and suppressed the notion of man as "person." When Hume, for example, set about to develop his "science" of human nature he found it impossible, in view of his phenomenalism, to develop in any adequate fashion what it means in truly empirical terms to be a person. How disappointing therefore to find that man in Hume's view is no more than a collection of his transitory states. Yet we should not be too hard on Hume, for even if we go all the way back to Boethius in the fifth century A.D. we hardly find it satisfactory to discover

147

6

that a person is "an individual substance of a rational nature." Though the formula contains a measure of truth, it falls far short either as a description or a "definition" of the reality of man as person.

No doubt the task of exploring in depth the meaning of "person" is one that is reserved for the philosophers of our times, if only they have the courage to meet the challenge at hand. But how is this challenge to be met? Not in my view by resorting to a method of analytic reductionism whereby the reality of the person dissolves before our eyes. The only method, as I see it, whereby the person as person can be manifested in the full uniqueness of his being, is by our coming to know him in his dynamic inter-relationship with other persons. This is to say that if we are to discover man as person, we must view him not as a static entity who does no more than occupy a certain "place" in the hierarchy of being: rather, we must discover man for all that he is, in radically empirical terms, by seeing how he acts in the company of his fellowmen.

Lest the reader imagine that I am substituting at this point a mere sociology of man for a genuine metapsychology in the sense of a true metaphysics of man, I wish to make it clear that what I am opposing is not an understanding of the person in the depths of his being, but any attempt which would seek to discover the person in a state of isolation from one's fellowman. Though I do not go all the way with Marcel when he states that "esse est coesse"—to be is to be with others—I fully appreciate the significance of what he is trying to say, which is this: the living reality of the person is one that grows and develops in the interaction that takes place— especially in a relation of love—*with other persons.*[3]

3. Marcel's philosophy of interpersonal relationships has received

Incarnational Philosophy: What Is It?

Here it is not merely a question of noetically discovering ourselves in the presence of other persons. It is a question rather of knowing that it is in and through our relationships with others that we, as persons, either expand by a process of maturity or decline by a process of decay. Let me make my point clear. Granting that we possess a certain natural equipment at birth for becoming what we are as adults, the fact of the matter is that the true actuality of ourselves as persons does not fully eventuate until and unless we learn to grow in the presence of the "other."

Neither must it be thought in the manner of Sartre, that the other is a kind of monster that blocks the path to the growth of my own subjectivity. Far from it. It is in and through the other, regarded not as "object" and not as "function" but *as person* who exists "sui generis" (in and for himself), that I am led on to an appreciation of myself.

Let us synopsize what we have been trying to say. Man is not the kind of being who can look at himself, narcissistically, if you will, and in the process, discover *himself*. Rather, we discover ourselves in the way we interact with others. But this is not all. It is in and through our relations with others that we ourselves grow and develop as persons. In our previous chapters I spoke of the meaning of self-transcendence, and what I have to say now is this: man is nothing unless he can transcend himself, first on the level of knowledge, but more especially on the level of love. But what does it mean to love another person?

Clearly not to regard that person as a function or to use him as an object or an instrument. One cannot, for example,

considerable prominence, especially in the decade of the sixties. For a fairly complete presentation of his philosophy, see G. Marcel, **The Mystery of Being** (Chicago: Henry Regnery Co., 1960), 2 vols. See also his **Homo Viator** (Chicago: Henry Regnery Co., 1951).

love a prostitute as such. To love the "other" is rather *to identify oneself with the interests of the other as though those interests* (desires, hopes, and the like) *were one's own.* This is the meaning of self-transcendence as love. But let us return to our central point. The person as person grows and develops in a dynamic interrelationship with other persons. Here, however, we must not allow ourselves to be carried away as though to imagine that *every* relationship to the other is conducive to psychological growth. Only on the condition that we do in fact identify with the interests of the other does any real personal development take place.

In other words, at the moment we begin to use other persons for our own ends we debase not only the other, but also, by implication, ourselves, and to that extent we become less of a person. Suppose you swindle your neighbor out of two thousand dollars with the promise of a service that you fail to provide. In so doing you become inauthentically related to the "other"; in which case the only value of the other is, not himself as person, but his money.

But what if you hire someone for his services on the basis of a *quid pro quo*? Is there anything personal about such a transaction as this? Clearly not, if you regard the person you hire as a slave. To treat anyone as a slave is obviously to depersonalize the inherent worth of the "other" as person, to violate his dignity as a man. Yet merely to hire one for his services is not to treat him as a slave, since the person in question acts as a free agent in the sense that he can either accept your offer or reject it. Yet even when he accepts your offer he does so with the dignity of a person who has done so on the basis of a personal choice.

One other point. Many persons regard themselves as capable of aspiring after fine ideals. It is no trivial truth, however, that the "proof lies in the pudding." From the

150

point of view of a truly incarnational philosophy, we do not love the other unless we love him in the flesh, which is to say, in all the circumstances, good and bad, of his life as we find it. The "proof lies in the pudding" in the sense that the real test of our love of the other is that we love him as he is, and not according to some romanticized version of him or her as created in our own imagination. Parents, for example, who love their children only while the children are asleep, possess a dubious love indeed, and well has William James remarked that some persons have a profound admiration of abstract justice and generosity. Yet all too often does this admiration decline when we meet these qualities in the street because, as he puts it, the circumstances make them vulgar.

Conclusion

The inner life of man is such that it grows and develops not in isolation from the world, but incarnationally in a dynamic relationship with others. To acknowledge this vital truth is to imply, as we have stated in the earlier part of this chapter, that man is no mere biological continuum, but spirit and organism in one; and it is the life of the spirit that "quickens," if you will, the life of the organism.

In such a view man is the kind of being who is constantly seeking not merely to control his environment, but to *transcend himself*. Moreover, he achieves this self-transcendence by a constant striving in a world of persons, toward a realm of spiritual values that are just as real, if not more so, than the bread we eat. Not by bread alone does man live, but by sharing his bread and his wisdom and his life with other men. Here, then, lies the key, or at least one of the central avenues to happiness: to grow and develop as person by participating fully and in a spirit of benevolence, in the life of the "other" as though the interests of the other were identical with our own.

The *sickness* of modern man is the sickness of his having removed himself, in an abstract and impersonal society, from those relationships which alone can make him grow. In view of this fact there is only one path to which he can return if he is to regain his sanity, and this is the path of love. In the chapter that follows I should like to open to the reader some insights that may help him to grasp in its yet fuller meaning, the therapy of love.

Too, as a final note I want to make clear to the reader my awareness of the deeper theological meaning of the term "incarnational" as it refers to the extremely important relationship that philosophy bears to the doctrine of the Incarnation in the strict and proper sense of the term. While the application of philosophy to this doctrine falls outside the scope of this chapter, let me say that the fullest meaning of love cannot be achieved on the level of philosophy alone unless we are willing to settle for a purely philanthropic love of our fellow-man. The highest dimension of Love is to be found on the theological level of Charity as a Love that pertains directly to God and which under that same formality reaches out to one's fellow man. While philosophy therefore cannot of itself attain to such a love, it should at least be open to it, and given this higher dimension, at least do what it can to prepare the way.

10

SIMPLICITY
AND THE
WAY OF THE
EMOTIONS

*Introductory
Remark*

Up to this
point we have seen the futility of any attempt to deny the
ultimately metaphysical nature of man. Too, in however a
capsule form, we have seen the inadequacy of all the voluntarisms of the past few decades insofar as man is a creature
of intelligence as well as of will. Finally, in the course of our
attempt to use metapsychology as a kind of therapy for
modern man, we have traced out man's fundamental desire
for meaning in terms both of the desire and the need for
transcendence, and in our last chapter we have seen how it
is possible for man to transcend himself, not by a reversion
to one of the spiritualisms of the past, but by a total re-
evaluation of man as spiritual organism. Nothing less than
an incarnational philosophy can provide an authentic basis
for the liberation of the human spirit.

This being said, it remains for us now to examine in
greater detail how the life of man—as incarnational spirit—
can mature and develop only with the growth of what we
shall call the "higher emotions." What these higher emotions
are and how they are related as therapy to the life of the
human spirit is in part the burden of our present chapter.

The Modern Situation: A Resumé

Let us begin with a bold assertion: modern man became disorientated because of a certain amnesia of the spirit. For want of self-knowledge and a true love of self he has become a traitor to himself. Through force of habit, a habit imposed on him by the trivialities of modern life, he has abrogated his human intelligence to matters of secondary import, as though the primary ones were of negligible concern. Having repressed the demands of his higher nature, he has given full play to his irrational impulses and to the tyranny of the senses. Finally, having adopted pragmatism as a way of life, modern man has lost his capacity for anything beyond the level of pure sensory enjoyment, and in the process has failed to appreciate persons as persons and things as things, except from the point of view of their use.

No doubt the immediate response to this situation is the desire to seek out a cure. Unfortunately, however, there is no cure in the sense in which many persons would look for it. There is no panacea. This situation, however, does not prevent us from looking for the *direction* in which a cure lies, the direction which points to the need for simplicity, the need for man's becoming like a child again. I do not, of course, wish to exaggerate this truth, this need, but the point is simply that modern man has become so overladen with the sophistications of contemporary life as to have abandoned the search for the authentic. Society, in other words, has so conditioned man to certain modes of inauthentic behavior as to lead to an amnesia of the basic needs of the spirit. The problem, then, is to diagnose, in a yet fuller sense than in our previous chapters, the source of the disease in the hope of providing later the kind of therapy that is needed.

154

Simplicity and Emotions

The Human Intelligence and Its Fundamental Needs

In earlier chapters I have referred repeatedly to modern subjectivism as the sort of thing that has all but atrophied man's power to think for himself in terms, not of introspective analysis, but of *being,* and herein lies the initial loss of simplicity, that is, on the level of the human intelligence. If indeed, man is to recover his sanity on the level of action he must first recover it on the level of thought, and doing this involves a reconditioning of the human intelligence to an understanding of the basic truths that it is naturally destined to know, such as the fundamental truth that reality, including the reality of human life itself, when viewed from the proper perspective, does make some kind of sense.

But let us reinforce our point as to the subjectivism of modern life. Under the influence of the long-standing tradition of the so-called empiricism of Hume and the transcendental idealism of Kant, modern man has inherited a tradition, reinforced by the errors of psychology, in which he has become entwined, so to speak, in the labyrinthine ways of his own mind. Under the impact of subjective idealism and cultural relativism he has lost his fundamental capacity to think and to judge—in realistic terms—about himself and the world in which he lives. He is the captive of the inner world of his own subjective categories, of a make-believe world that has deprived him of the realism which under normal conditions is part of his natural inheritance.

To make my point clear, the problem with man today is not one of his failure to use psychology, but of his failure to use anything else that would put him in dynamic contact with the real. Instead of cultivating, as his nature requires him to do, *an ontology of values that is based on the realities of life,* he has allowed himself to become literally overwhelmed by psychology, thus falling heir to the delusion that the perfect understanding of the self lies, frequently in combination with all sorts of drugs, in an all-consuming introspective habit of mind.

Introspection in the sense I speak of it here is a way of life that detracts from man's essential orientation to the world of primitive nature and to the world of other persons understood in depth and as existing in their own right. This is to say that introspection so understood is an overriding habit of mind that perverts the human intelligence from its natural use and prevents it from establishing a rich and beneficial contact with the world outside. While it may therefore be of some value for everyone to know something of psychology, it is an abnormal state of affairs to find a society, such as our own, in which the categories of psychology, abnormal psychology in particular, have become so all-pervasive that the world outside tends to recede in the background.[1]

Simplicity and the Tower of Babel

This much for now concerning the loss of simplicity on the level of the natural intelligence. It is enough, for a rough diagnosis, to know that modern man has deprived himself, in the order of knowledge, of those simple truths which even a child can grasp with the proper disposition of mind. But let us pass on, however briefly, to another level involving the loss of simplicity, the level of human speech.

1. Too, I have always felt that there is something essentially morbid in everyone's taking, so to speak, an inordinate, prurient interest in the details both of medical science and in the details of the "science of the mind." It is one thing to be well-informed, but quite another to become obsessively preoccupied with pathological details.

Simplicity and Emotions

No one will doubt, of course, that the "communications arts" have reached an unprecedented point of development, whether through the medium of the telephone, radio, television, outer-space communications, and so on. But the point to grasp is this: in proportion as the "communications arts" grow and develop modern man seems to lose the *capacity for the kind of speech that comes directly to the point,* for the kind of speech that goes directly *to the heart of reality. More often than not speech becomes a cover-up for our inmost thoughts rather than a method of revealing them.* Especially in the advertising world, words are used not to inform the prospective consumer of the merits of the product at hand, but to mislead, to cajole, and even outrightly to deceive. Likewise in the educational world, "academicians," especially in our schools of education, go to ridiculous extremes in inventing a jargon that is intelligible to no one, including themselves; and this in the hope of giving the appearance of "science" to what in point of fact is nothing but a nominalistic amalgam and contrivance of their own minds.[2] The problem today, then, as regards the loss of simplicity on the level of speech, is man's lack of

2. If it seems I have been too severe with the imperious demands of a commercial world that has dehumanized itself and its consumers, that is, through smooth speech that has covered up some bad habits of mind and heart, perhaps some finger of blame should also be cast—for different reasons—on the educational world as well. What I refer to is the dominant tendency within many of our schools of education and within the world of the academy at large to accept as fact the unfounded assumptions of a behaviorist psychology that has reduced man to a bundle of instincts and responses. In such a view speech, human speech, that is, is viewed only in terms of the responses it evokes, and **not in terms of the element of truth it is meant to convey.** In my view there is no single doctrine that reveals in more stark and inestimably harmful terms the "betrayal of wisdom."

ability to say "nay, nay" and "yes, yes" when such types of answers are called for.

Stoicism and Its Inhibiting Effects

I have spoken of the loss of simplicity on the level of intelligence and briefly also on the level of human speech. I wish to speak of it now in relation to the loss of the emotions in modern life. But before I do I want to say a few words on the inhibiting effects of stoicism as it relates to the life of contemporary man. By stoicism I mean any attempt whatsoever to repress the emotions at a time when they demand expression and full play. Stoicism has, of course, a long history, but its classical modern form is to be found in the duty ethics of Immanuel Kant.

In his *Metaphysics of Morals* Kant makes every attempt to establish the claim that the moral character of our actions derives from one source alone, namely, that we perform them from a motive of duty. This means that such emotions as love, hope, or joy, to the extent that they do serve as motives for the actions we perform, tend to derogate from the moral character of those acts. Carried to its utmost extreme, the hypothesis of Kant would mean, for example, that those actions which I perform for my wife, children, or country, are *less* moral to the extent that they are dominated not by a motive of duty, but by a motive of love.

Lest my criticism be misunderstood I want to make it clear to the reader that I am not impugning Kant's own motive in his attempt to establish an *absolute* system of morals. Compared to much of the *a*morality that prevails in society today, the ethics of Kant, especially with his insistence on the inviolability of the person and of his need to act as though his action were a rule for the whole of mankind,

158

such an ethics is like a breath of fresh air. However, my own criticism of Kant is basically in agreement with Schopenhauer's as to the ultimate constitutive motive of the morality of human acts. I would far prefer Schopenhauer's motive of love (of *Mitleid*) over the duty ethics of Immanuel Kant—without, of course, rejecting the motive of duty altogether. Duty has a role in ethics, and a very important one at that, but not the predominant or exclusive role attributed to it by Kant.

This much, however, for the ethics of Kant, which disallows or diminishes the experience of the emotions—higher or lower—in the conduct of one's moral life. Few persons, of course, today are as strongly impelled by a motive of duty as they were at the time of Kant. What they do hold in common, however, with the ethics of the Kantian critique, is an outlook of mind which suppresses the values of the emotions, especially the higher emotions, in the life of modern man. The modern outlook is such that man today must "hem himself in" in order in some fashion "to protect himself." In a word, the capital sin of modern life is for any person to be so unsophisticated and naive as to wear his emotions "on his sleeve," and it is precisely in this sense that we speak of the stoicism of modern life.

Apropos of the need for simplicity, the hypothesis I wish to state is simply this: *it is the failure on the part of modern man to develop and express his emotions, especially the higher ones, that has led him into the psychological morass into which he has sunk.* Every man, will it or not, is plagued with the search for meaning. This search, however, is futile if it is pursued, as it were, on a purely cerebral level, on the level of noninvolvement and in the vacuum of one's own conscious states. The search for meaning in other words, in view of the total nature of man, is just as much a social affair as it is an attempt on the part of the individual to "find himself" by some magical process of introspective analysis alone.

But let me come yet closer to the point. The problem with modern man is that he has lost the sense of what William James has called "passional nature." I do not mean this, of course, in a narrow sense, on the level of sex, but rather in terms of man's reluctance, if not his inability, to develop his higher emotions both in relation to his own needs and those of his fellowmen. The problem is that of the failure, due to the atrophy of emotion, to achieve for oneself and for others a certain simplicity of life. It is the failure, as we have already explained it, to achieve self-transcendence.

Held back, as it were, by a kind of pseudo-consciousness of the self, modern man too often relegates himself to a truncated form of existence, to a kind of half-existence whereby the higher emotions, to say nothing of such things as the expression of anger when it is called for, are sealed off in a self-contained vacuum. And the villain of the piece is nothing less than what we have already spoken of as the pragmatism of modern life: too many persons simply do not wish to become involved except for the limited objective of "winning friends" and "influencing people" to their own ends. In this sense modern life is characterized by a habit of mind whereby one deliberately avoids conflicts, arguments and involvements, while retaining all along, *on the surface,* the niceties and courtesies of one's daily and professional life.

A moment ago I made a passing reference to the emotion of anger. Let me briefly explain the intent of my remark. While anger is not a "higher" emotion, there are times, especially in the face of evil or injustice, when a person *should* be aroused, at least to the point of doing something about it. It is essentially an inhuman, depersonalized mode of response when a person in the face of injustice is willing simply to "stand by." This phenomenon of non-involvement has been highlighted in recent magazines in the portrayal of those situations where dozens of people, as bystanders, allow themselves to witness a crime without even calling the police.

My chief concern, however, is not with the problem of anger as such, but much more so with the positive emotions of hope, love, and joy. No need here for a scholastic disputation on the abstract qualities of these emotions. Everyone knows, if only through vicarious experiences, the meaning of each of these emotions. Thus hope is the confident expectation that some future event will take place in the absence of any guarantee that it will. Love is the absorption in a "project" that is good for someone other than ourselves. Joy is a sense of elation in the fullness of the present moment without a worrisome concern that that moment soon will be past.

This much, however, by way of analysis. The point of our inquiry is to discern the measure of suffering—in psychic terms—that results from the failure to lead a well-balanced emotional life. Some people, of course, do get "carried away" with their emotions. They are flighty, they wear their emotions "on their sleeve." But in a deeper sense, unless one *is* carried away by an emotion, it is questionable whether he benefits from it at all. But let us relate all of this to the need for a recovery of simplicity. Simplicity on the level of the emotions is a disposition of soul that enables one to react without any particular worry of how absurd or ridiculous we might appear to other persons who may not understand our own state of mind. It means that we are completely honest, on the level of the emotions, in our reaction to a situation or event as given, and not as reflected upon by an introspective habit of mind.

No doubt the reader will caution me at this point as to the necessity of reserve, nor am I unmindful of my insistence in an earlier chapter on the centrality of prudence in our lives. However, the problem of modern life, as far as the higher emotions are concerned, is not generally a lack of reserve, but that of an inhibiting stoicism which prevents their authentic development. In any event, it is good to know that prudence is not only the virtue of caution, but the command of reason itself, enjoining us, whenever the need exists, to take the necessary risks, including whatever risks are necessary for the development of our emotional life. Trite as the saying may be, it is better to love and have lost than not to have loved at all—though ideally it is best for all men to love wisely.

The Emotions and Their Cognitive Value

Intellectualism and voluntarism, these are the poles toward which modern philosophy has swerved as opposite points of the needle without any adequate means of resolving the tension between the two. Leibnitz, for one, is the classical example of an "extreme intellectualist" or rationalist for whom the whole of reality is, in the manner of his pre-established harmony, like the unwinding of a cosmological clock. In such a world view there is little room for surprises, chance, or freedom. At the other end of the pole are all the will-type philosophies, like the pragmatism of William James, in which the will-to-believe (or some other type of will) takes precedence over any claim on the part of the intellect to know what *is*, independently of our willing it to be so.

Simplicity and Emotions

The position I am developing in this book is one which seeks to avoid these extremes. It is a position which points in the direction of what I have already called an integral realism, a realism that takes fully into account, toward a true philosophy of action, the values both of intelligence and will. Lest it be thought, however, that man is a creature either of intelligence or will by themselves (or of both together), we must at this point relate our theory of the higher emotions to the yet fuller development of the realism of which I spoke but a moment ago. Integral realism, both as an epistemological theory and as a psychological fact, is based on the view that knowledge, especially as understanding of life *(intellectus vitae)*, significantly derives from more than one source. In other words, *a true philosophic realism is open to every segment and dimension of reality that is in any way whatsoever open to the mind and heart of man.*

No one will doubt, of course, that the intellect of man— what Jacques Barzun has called the "house of intellect"— is an independent source of knowledge. Admittedly also, regarding certain types of knowledge like chemistry, physics, and so on, intellect alone will suffice to produce the desired effect of coming to grips with a certain segment of reality. Our own concern at the moment, however, is to show that there are other types of knowledge, at least equally as genuine as science, that carry man on, noetically, past the sphere of scientific knowledge as such and into the realm of the spirit.

What I am trying to suggest is the falsity of the positivist hypothesis (too often assumed by philosophers) which sets up a disjunction in hard and fast terms between values and facts as though values themselves were not a certain kind of fact. This is to say that the higher values of life—

spiritual, cultural, and moral—provide us with a contact with reality that ordinary facts do not. In so doing, these values bring with them, in the language of St. Thomas Aquinas, a kind of *knowledge by connaturality* in the sense that we can distinguish *through intimate personal experience* and *through the path of emotional involvement*, the authentic from the meretricious, the true from the false. This latter kind of knowledge, far from being autonomous and unrelated to the purpose of life, brings with it an understanding of life *(intellectus vitae)* that academic knowledge alone cannot achieve.

Take the literary artist as an example. Only up to a point can it be said that a novelist remains detached from his characters as the actual telling of his story depends in large measure on the intensity of his own emotional experience. Clearly no novelist can produce a living experience for his reader unless he himself has initially undergone the same type of experience for himself. What is yet more important, however, is the fact that a great novelist can, through the medium of his art, bring the reader to a level of truth about the drama and the crisis of life that is simply unattainable by pure scientific means. Although great novels therefore may be fictional in content, they are in their symbolic meaning and reference a source, not only of inspiration and life, *but of the very truth of life itself.*

In a similar vein I want to apply what I have been saying to the realm of philosophy, and it is this: in the tradition of Moses Maimonides (1135-1204), creative thinking in philosophy is not stimulated by vicarious issues—by solutions to meaningless problems—but by those issues that are of greatest concern in our personal life. Hence, philosophers do not generally expend their power and

164

passion unless they are themselves affected by the problems of life, and what matters most of all for the fruitful and creative development of philosophy is that the philosopher himself undergo in his own way a kind of dark night of the soul. *Great philosophers in other words, are the emergent products of the crises of the human spirit.* Insofar, then, as every philosopher needs a motive that impels him to toil and to sweat for the truth, it is no exaggeration to say that philosophy in its best and higher sense as *personal wisdom* is in a limited sense for each philosopher a kind of *apologia pro vita sua.*[3]

But let us return to our central point: it is a mistaken conception to imagine that the habit of critical thinking should set up a disjunction, a rupture, between values and facts. As we have already noted (and I refer especially to the higher values of life), values themselves are a certain kind of fact, of the sort which in order to be known must in some measure be experienced within the overall context of life itself. While it is one thing therefore for a professor in a classroom to denigrate the values, let us say, of a religious way of life, it is quite another for a person committed to those same values both to experience them in their primitive flavor and to derive from them, both psychologically and ontologically, the measure of enrichment they afford.

On this last point I cannot sufficiently emphasize the dangers of an excessively analytical habit of mind which isolates values from life and subjects them to a kind of

---

3. Here, I do not mean to suggest, of course, that all you need to understand a philosopher is to psychoanalyze the motives that engendered his work. The work of philosophy proper is an objective inquiry into truth; yet the motives which impel the philosopher to search out the truth are of the utmost concern.

anatomical dissection whereby even those values of the
highest order tend to dissolve before our very eyes. It is
not on the level of abstract analysis that values can be
known for what they are in terms of their ontological
referents. What we have been trying to say therefore is
this: *emotional experience, if it is genuinely such and in
harmony with our rational powers, has a cognitive value
of its own that is impossible to achieve by purely rational
or scientific means.*

The Alleged Antithesis of Mind and Heart

No doubt the reader is reminded at this point of that
famous saying of Pascal's to the effect that the heart has
reasons of which the mind is quite unaware. I do not, of
course, side in with the fideistic voluntarism of Blaise
Pascal (1623-1662), but I readily concede that he makes
a good point if by the "heart" we mean to symbolize certain aspects of our emotional experience. I should want to
assert that herein lies an authentic source of knowledge,
as *intellectus vitae,* provided we make no effort to *detach*
the heart from the mind. No need here, in other words,
to allow a completely autonomous function to our purely
emotional experience as though it were divorced from its
roots in intelligence. As a matter of fact, an *integral realism*
demands a proper balance between emotional experience
as such and the life of the mind. For example, hope as an
emotional experience is a virtue, a point of strength, provided we have some known object to hope for in the
absence of which it becomes nothing more than illusion.

Be this as it may, it is well to note here what Charles
Sanders Peirce has stated in an altogether different context, namely, that we should "not pretend to doubt in

philosophy what we do not doubt in our hearts."[4] What Peirce had in mind in context was the inauthentic character of the Cartesian doubt as to the reality of the outside world. But let us apply these words in the yet wider context of the life of man as a whole. To doubt the whole realm of moral and spiritual values on the dubious methodological grounds that they are not susceptible to a kind of narrow "empirical" test is to my way of thinking the height of "philosophical" stupidity. It is a kind of foolishness that marks the cult of unwisdom in our times.

Such an approach to philosophy results not only in the atrophy of the powers of the spirit; it is the very antithesis to the notion of philosophy as a kind of wisdom that is open to truths of a yet higher order than itself, namely, the orders of religious truth as based on divine revelation. Not only, then, should we *not* doubt what we do not doubt in our hearts, but we should bend every effort of attention *to cup the flame* of those higher truths that are imbedded, however fleetingly so, in the conduct of our daily lives; and this regardless of whether these same truths are susceptible to the methods of a logical type of analysis or not.

Psychologism and Its Baneful Effects

More than once have I made a reference in this volume to "psychologism." By the use of this term I mean an overweening habit of mind which reduces all values to the category of a purely subjective experience taken as such. To the person infected with this habit—be he psychologist or not—all values are mere projections of im-

4. **Collected Papers,** 5.265.

pulse in the manner of the Freudian "explanation" of God as an "objectification" of a subliminal "father image." This, at any rate, is what I mean by psychologism, and the point is to show that it is precisely such a habit of mind which leads to a subjectivism in philosophy from which there is no point of return. Once it is asserted or implied that all values are rooted in a kind of wishful thinking the only remaining alternative is that of a return to the relativism of Protagoras, for whom man himself, whether he consciously wills it or not, is the measure of all things.

Psychologism, then, is a revival in a peculiarly modern form, of the relativism of the sophists, and it is a kind of sophistry which refuses to meet a given datum—in this case a datum of life itself—on its own unique terms and for its own worth. No doubt all values are subjective in the basic sense that they need to be *appropriated* by the one who adopts them, *but it is a peculiar type of axiological reductionism that attempts to explain, along the lines of the "genetic fallacy," all values in terms of their psychological origin alone.*

What I am trying to suggest therefore is that there are certain values which men share in common, not because of custom alone, but because the things they represent are good in themselves. Consider, for example, the inherent dignity of the person. Is it only through custom or some kind of psychological projection that we commonly refuse, in spite of Schopenhauer's opinion, to regard persons only as means and insist on treating them as ends-in-themselves? With reference to this or any number of examples, is it not absurd to suppose that things, all things, are good only because we deem them to be so? And is it not the case rather that there are certain things (like the value of the human person) which we deem to be good because they

168

are good in themselves and therefore worthy of the value that we attach to them in our personal lives?

To admit that such *is* the case is to imply, on the one hand, the falsity of any axiological positivism whereby all values are placed on an equal plane, the plane of our *willing* them to be so, and to admit, on the other hand, as we have been trying to show, that some values at least have an ontological foundation, or in quite simple words, a basis in fact. It is a part therefore of an integral realism and a radical empiricism of the spirit, to acknowledge these fundamental truths that axiological voluntarists are so quick to deny.

Most emphatically, then, the viewpoint I reject is the position of those philosophers and psychologists who maintain that the emotional life of man is purely unrelated to the life of the mind. In defense of the position I have taken, let it be stated unequivocally, as a case in point, that love (as a typical example of one of the higher emotions) is not, contrary to the popular axiom, blind. Admittedly love as infatuation (and this is an abuse of the term) can readily distort our judgment, but this is no more than an aberration of love in its authentic sense. True love, as an efficacious willing of that which is really good for the "other" leads, *in the objective order*, to an understanding of the good qualities in a person, qualities that could not be discovered, at least in their full depth, by any other means.

What we are trying to suggest therefore, is that love, as well as all of the higher emotions like joy, hope, and contentment, have a quality of *synthesis* about them which leads to a higher type of knowledge of the "object" that no amount of analysis would reveal. In this connection too, I wish to remind my reader of the profound statement (quoted in an earlier chapter) that truth, as William James expressed it, is ultimately that which integrates our lives. Divorced from the pragmatism that underlies it, this saying expresses exactly what I mean when I submit that the higher emotions have a cognitive value that is otherwise beyond human reach.

Unfortunately, many persons who would agree to this statement on the level of their personal experience would hesitate, by virtue of their positivist leaning, to write it into their philosophy of life. Yet the fact remains that science, genuine knowledge that it is, is not the only pathway to the real. The real is a multileveled affair, and there are as many different approaches to the real as there are avenues of noetic experience. What is important therefore for purposes of an integral realism is to know that emotional experience— properly understood and properly gauged—can and does give us a measure of insight into reality that would otherwise be hidden from our eyes.

Concluding Remarks

In the light of all we have said it should be clear that the higher emotions, far from throwing up a smokescreen between mind and reality, are themselves a source of knowledge that leads to an understanding of life. To repress these emotions, whether on the level of art, morality, or religion, is to reduce man to a shadow of himself, and it is exactly this habit of repression that has produced many of the disorders that characterize modern life. Apropos therefore of the value of philosophy as therapy let it be clearly stated that a truly radical empiricism is an empiricism of the spirit as well as one of the mind and the senses. Moreover, "realism" as we speak of it in philosophy must carry us beyond the bold assertion that the external world is real, that it exists. What is far more important is that man come to know reality on the level of his experiential contact with it, through his power of emotion as well as through his power of intellect and will.

Finally, a full-fledged commitment to the higher values of life will serve *as nothing else can* to eradicate that deadly habit of mind whereby synthetic wholes are reduced to atomic particles that are emptied of all meaning and content. The meaning of life, if it is to be perceived at all must be perceived on the level of synthesis and gestalt and not on the level of the kind of anatomical dissection whereby the "idea" of God, soul, person, or what have you, is reduced precisely to the status of an "idea." If, therefore, modern man is to return to a condition of health he must at once abandon on the theoretical plane the kind of positivist reductionism of which we spoke in this essay, and on the practical level he must reject that false asceticism of modern life which makes all life a burden rather than a joy.

11

CONTEMPLA-
TION:
A LOST ART?

*Introductory
Remarks*

IN OUR ATTEMPT
to show the relevancy of philosophy to our times we have
come a long way, the way of showing the need of a total
reconstruction in philosophy, not along the lines of some new
type of system-building, in the grand style of Descartes or
Hegel, but along the lines of a new approach which I have
alternatively referred to as integral realism and a radical
empiricism of the spirit. A true and authentic philosophy is,
after all, an expression of the life of the mind, and where the
life of the mind is in a state of degeneration or decay, philosophy itself gravitates in the direction of scepticism, agnosticism, and the inauthentic modes of empiricism.

The problem therefore is to regenerate philosophy in such
a way that it will re-establish its relation to life, both to the
life of the mind and of the spirit, and this at a time of the
world's greatest need for philosophy. Such a revival, however, cannot come about until and unless the habitual
modesty of the American temperament abandons its confinement to the narrowing influence of pragmatism. In plain
language, the time has come to get beyond pragmatism
as an American philosophy of life. The time has come to

172

prepare for a more mature form of philosophy in the direction of an integral realism.

Action and Contemplation: The Need for a Restoration of Balance

Integral realism, as I visualize it, is a way of philosophic thinking which from one important point of view seeks to restore the balance between action and contemplation. But to this the reader may reply: "All well and good, but first convince me that 'contemplation' (in whatever sense you employ the term) has any relevance to modern life at all." Or more basically, "What do you mean by 'contemplation'?" Pragmatism aside, the question is, of course, legitimate, and not only legitimate but necessary. To many, if not most persons today, 'contemplation' suggests by implication a kind of narcissism, involving a withdrawal from the real world of persons and things and entailing, of necessity, what Dewey has called an 'otiose' habit of mind. Yet barring such misconceptions as these, our interest is to show that contemplation (properly understood) is not only a respectable occupation for man but one of his greatest needs.

No doubt everyone is aware these days that the habit of contemplation is one of the distinguishing marks of most Oriental cultures and, in a vague sense, that perhaps "Western man" has in this respect something to learn from the East. My own interest, however, is to get beyond such vague generalities as these in the hope of defining in more exact terms the meaning of contemplation. Contemplation, which I regard for the most part as a "lost art," is not either literally or figuratively something "out of this world," and the sooner we shake off this notion the better prepared will we be to appreciate its true worth. As I see it, contemplation

173

is not a method of retreat or escape from the world, but rather, a means of confrontation with the real, and what I have in mind is this: action and contemplation are not, as it were, incompatible modes of activity, but complementary aspects of one total coin. This is to say that contemplation is not a kind of "sitting back" or "lying still" in order to daydream about reality, but rather, a method or mode of reflection on the meaning of what is given in experience. It is, if you will, a kind of "reading between the lines" of our activities by which in a spirit of reflection we grasp, however partially, the ciphers and pointers of our experience.

On the Development of Aisthesis

But let us begin our analysis on a yet more elementary plane—on the level of the senses. I have long maintained that the habit of contemplation—whether on a philosophical, artistic, or religious level—is dependent fundamentally on the activity of the senses. The difficulty of understanding this point is aggravated by the fact that our senses these days are dulled and jaded by too great a proliferation of noise and visual images on all sides. The dullness has reached such a point that man has forgotten—in a sensate culture[1] —how to use his senses in a manner that satisfies his soul. To catch the brunt of my meaning I ask the reader to learn something about the lost art of contemplation from a child who, without any sophistication, knows how to absorb himself for hours in the simplest objects of experience, like a toy, a ring, or a rope. Have you ever watched children, completely oblivious to the passage of time, play games for

1. I am indebted for the use of this term to Petirim Sorokin's **The Crisis of our Age** (New York: E. P. Dutton, 1941).

174

hours on end with no trace of boredom or fatigue?

No doubt many a harrassed mother will say this is no more than a dream, but truth to tell, it is a fact that anyone can observe for himself if he is willing to take the time to do so. But let us not quibble: the point I wish to convey is that "aesthetics" in the root meaning of the term (as a derivative from the Greek word "aisthesis") means, not some highly specialized method of appreciating beautiful works of art, but simply "sense perception." *The problem is not to make all men artists but to discover the artist in all men.* To perceive with the senses in such a way as to explore the meaning of objects or simply to play with them, is to my mind the basic meaning of contemplation. There is no question of the fact that the senses *do* have a biological use, but the *use* of the senses has been so much exaggerated in modern society that their most basic function as knowledge and enjoyment has all but been placed in the background.

As a starting point, then, let us say this: before we can restore the act of contemplation to its yet higher planes, we must first come to appreciate it on the level of sense perception. This means above all that everyone should learn to recapture the lost gift of childhood—the pleasure of "aisthesis"—as a sensible appreciation and enjoyment of the simple objects of our experience. It means that we recapture the simple joy of smelling roses, of observing the formation of clouds, of noting the change in color of far away mountains, of finding expressions of love, hate, joy, and sadness in the faces of our fellowmen.

Doing this, of course, runs counter to the grain of modern life which is so pervasively slanted in the direction of efficiency and control as to lose sight of the value of taking time out to discover the values of persons and things as they are in themselves. The problem today is, of course, a lack of leisure, considered not from the viewpoint of time, but from a viewpoint of a habit of mind that acts and reflects in disregard of the element of time.[2] In other words, we have become for the most part a nation of clock-watchers whose chief concern in life is not the occupation of the moment, but the need to be "on schedule" for whatever occupation that follows. Once a measure of leisure is provided we become, out of force of habit, restless and neurotic because none of the occupations of the moment are sufficient to absorb our attention.

In view, then, of those ingrained habits of mind and of life which make a contemplative approach to reality all but a dream, the first thing we must do is to show how and why the habit of contemplation rightly understood can be a tonic for the crippling disorders of modern life. Yet before modern man can be taught the *how* of a contemplative approach to reality he must first be convinced of its need.

The Need for Interiorization

More than once in the course of this volume I have warned against the danger of a too purely introspective habit of mind. The problem with too many persons today is that they are too much wrapped up in themselves for failure, as we have already shown elsewhere, to achieve a measure of self-transcendence. Let it not be imagined, however, that "introspection" and "interiorization" are in any sense synonymous terms.

By "interiorization" I mean a habit of mind whereby a

2. See Josef Pieper's incomparable little work, **Leisure, The Basis of Culture** (New York: Pantheon Books, 1952), trans. by A. Dru.

person comes into possession of himself, not from the selfish point of view of a preoccupation with his own concerns,
but from the point of view of his coming to know reality on
a yet deeper plane. Let us draw up a picture of an "interior"
man. He is one who seldom allows himself to become so
spread out in his external activities as to lose the "center"
of his own being, and it is indeed the "center of things"—
both within himself and without—that is the object of his
primary concern. More specifically, an "interior" man is one
who knows how to drink deeply of the joys of being by
himself in a posture of silence and of absorption in the
things of the spirit.

I do not mean, of course, to suggest a type of person
who at the drop of a hat can, as it were, "take leave of his
senses." Rather an "interior" man is one who uses his
senses, his emotions, his will, and his mind—indeed all the
powers of his being—to discover for himself *and to savor*
of the real meaning of life. But to do all this he must, above
all, create a certain kind of silence in his soul. To many
persons "silence" is a frightening word and the worst mis-
fortune that could happen to them is to be left completely
to themselves. Not so, however, for the person for whom
silence is something more than an emptiness or a blank.
Rather the person who seeks silence in a contemplative spirit
of mind does so in a manner that takes one beyond the realm
of concepts and images as such into one of quiet listening,
of a well-coordinated harmony of the powers of the soul.
This is to say that there must be something in every man of
the spirit of the monk, of the person who, in his moments of
reflection, gets beyond the surface events of everyday life
to a deeper understanding of what these events mean personally for him.

If I may digress for a moment, I should like to say that

given such a habit of mind, one directly opposed to sheer activism, many of the neuroses and conflicts of modern life would gradually begin to disappear. *The problem with many persons today is precisely their failure to identify what for them is the source of their neuroses and conflicts.* Too often neurotic individuals reproach themselves for not doing enough, let us say, in the way of helping their fellowman. The source of their problem, however, lies in not doing enough for *themselves* in the development of what I have called an ever-deepening sense of interiorization. But let us explore this concept in yet greater depth.

The great problem of many neurotics is that of "roleplaying." Not having established a sufficient depth of intensity in their own inner being, they find themselves in the presence of others playing the role of the conformist, of what David Riesman, the noted Harvard sociologist, has called the "outer-directed" man. The most obvious need for such persons as these is that of solving what modern psychologists have described as the "identity crisis"—but in a manner the psychologists themselves have failed to understand. The problem here is simply this: how best is it possible for any individual, to say nothing of the neurotic, to resolve the crisis of identity without resorting to perverse forms of introspection on the one hand, and on the other, to a pure method of "outer-directedness"?

The answer to this problem lies in the search for a true process of interiorization that can come about only through the development of a contemplative habit of mind. At this point, however, we again seem to "draw a blank" as again the question arises, "How does one learn to contemplate?" No doubt the "how to" mentality of modern life is prejudicial to an activity which, though perfectly natural in itself, seems clumsy and awkward to one who knows nothing of its meaning. In short, there is no easy path to contemplation except through the deliberately chosen methods of silence, detachment, and leisure.

Silence is necessary to produce the right kind of "atmosphere" or milieu; detachment, to re-lease the powers of the soul (forgive the medieval expression) for the grasp of a more interior view of the nature of life; and leisure, to enable one to relish the joy of the present moment. But let us not wander off into vague generalities when the question at hand is that of learning the true essence of the contemplative frame of mind.

May I suggest first of all that contemplation is, above all, an activity—not a productive activity, grant you, but one in which the "higher powers" of the individual person are fruitfully, though not gainfully, employed in the search of an object that can absorb that person. Whether any external results are visible or not, contemplation as an immanent activity is one in which psychologically a person is carried above and beyond the narrowness of his own self to a quasi-intuitive awareness of "the truths of life," one's relations to God, other persons, etc., etc. Unlike any other activity, however, contemplation is very little dependent on any conscious effort that involves a straining, a struggle, as it were, for the "object" which it seeks to possess; which is to say, that a certain attitude of aggressiveness is the kiss of death to one who seeks contemplation. The relation of the one who contemplates to the object of his contemplation is rather one of loving submission, of simple abandonment, of a kind of listening in which no attempt is made to *dominate* that which we seek to know and to love.

The title of this chapter speaks of contemplation as an "art." It is an art in the sense that in its beginning stages at least, a measure of practice is required for those who have

179

7

never developed the habit. Thus it is no easy matter for a busy executive who is accustomed to controlling people and events, to place himself in an environment and in a frame of mind where the usual paraphernalia of his occupation are withdrawn. More likely than not such a person feels as trapped as a bird in the cage and feels that there is nothing more to do than to twiddle his fingers till something more exciting comes along. Little does such a person realize the need for what Marcel has called "humility before being," as a necessary pre-condition for contemplation—a condition and a state of mind of which very few "practical" people are capable of developing, at least in a relatively short period of time.

Such, however, is the nature of contemplation that it is we who must allow ourselves, in the process of interiorization, to be dominated by the object rather than the other way around; and it is here that the difficulty lies. To the "practical" man the only thing that matters is to "take the situation in hand," to size up alternatives, and then grind out a decision. To a contemplative person, however, life is more simple than this in the sense that *there are many moments in his life when it is better not to act at all, but rather to abstain from acting in a posture of receptivity and silence to what is given.* Few persons realize that there is great wisdom in developing, as a counter-agent to pragmatism, a certain philosophy of not-acting.

Lest the picture I present seem in any way forbidding to my reader, I wish to return to one of my central points: many persons who fear contemplation would find in their attempt to recapture this "lost art" that it is the one thing of which they stand in greatest need. Even if at the time set aside one feels as dull as a vegetable, he will later discover that the fruits of contemplation, taken in the beginning as

180

an attitude of silence, are far more rewarding than anything that one would at first expect. This is why there is a need to recapture a contemplative spirit. I think it was Charles Lamb (1775-1834) who said something to this effect: "May the Lord who said that it is not good for man to be alone preserve me from the much greater evil of never having a moment to myself." Even, then, if you feel as dull as a vegetable at the moment you have gone off by yourself, remember that there is a certain kind of boredom that is good for the soul—the kind that completely reverses the rhythm of life's activities into one of leisurely enjoyment. In a word, there should be times in the life of all of us when we feel no particular need to "justify" ourselves in terms of an incessant round of activities, when the best thing we can do is to "waste" a generous amount of time on ourselves.

Obviously, then, the great remedy for the anxiety of modern life is the inner peace that is the result of this process of interiorization, and relevant to the point at hand is Martin Heidegger's (1899-   ) remark as to the distinction between anxiety and fear: fear has a definite object, anxiety does not. But *why* are people anxious? Not in many instances because of a felt need for something they definitely lack, let us say, a house or a car. Rather the source of anxiety is rooted in the need of the person to discover the very center of his being. Psychologists talk no end about people who feel uneasy about themselves and others with no clearly indicated reason as to why. Such persons are habitually "on edge" because they lack an interior source of motivation for the practical guidance of their lives. What is all important for such persons, then, is that they know how, gradually and over a period of time, to rediscover their authentic selves, and such rediscovery can take place only through the method of achieving an interior life.

Philosophy and Contemplation

We have come to the point of this chapter where it is necessary to review some of the highlights of this volume in relation to the subject at hand. Why, for example, has philosophy failed to provide the kind of guidance that is modern man's greatest need, let us say, to a well-ordered life and a well-ordered society? One level of answer to this question is to say that philosophy has withdrawn from the center of life by reason of its commitment to an excessively analytical habit of mind. *Analysis as hyperanalysis is equally as destructive of contemplation as is pragmatism as a way of life.* The problem with the analyst, of course, is that he is given to the habit of seeing only the parts of experience as parts, and seldom if ever as reconstructed wholes.[3] Yet it is precisely this aspect of contemplation which distinguishes it radically and essentially from any and all of the analytic modes of human cognition. In other words contemplation is neither itself an analytic type of thinking nor is it susceptible in the way that abstract logical thinking *is,* to an analysis of its "logical" parts. It is a way of looking at life and reality according to a "method" of its own—*which is a method of seeing things in their integral relationships as integral wholes* which are not (at the moment they are experienced) subject to a process of reflection. Accordingly, whenever in retrospect any attempt is made to analyze the

3. Whether they claim to be positivists or not, some analysts, to the extent that they become involved in this type of thinking, lie essentially within the tradition of a Humean type of empiricism which in spite of its name is a disguised form of rationalism in the sense that the only reality that exists is that which is susceptible to the overt inspection of our conscious reasoning power as such.

object of contemplation it all too often dissolves before our eyes *as though* it no longer exists.

What is important, therefore, for the philosophical analyst is to know, in regard to contemplative experience, the limitations of his own technique. Every attempt he makes at trying to understand the meaning of contemplation is, of course, commendable. But what he should know *as a philosopher* is the *radical difference that exists between cognition in its analytical and synthetic modes.* From the fact that one mode of thinking is in no way reducible to the other it would be a serious mistake, a mistake of methodology, to deny that the other exists. If therefore it is in any way granted that contemplation is either a distinct or even a higher mode of cognition which transcends the ordinary categories of a purely logical type of analysis, one's reaction should be, not to deny the validity of this type of experience, but to allow the uniqueness of its value for the conduct of human life.

One should not, however, be too hard on the analyst because the great culprit, concerning the "death" of philosophy as wisdom, is the psychological reductionist whose sole concern, if it exists at all, is to examine the *conditions* of contemplation—philosophical, artistic, religious—in total disregard of any objective foundation on which it might be based. *It is one thing, of course, to treat contemplation phenomenologically by way of "bracketing" its ontological meaning, but quite another to reduce contemplation to its purely psychological molds.* Such a procedure is equivalent to the assertion that there is no possibility of a relationship between the object as contemplated and the object as it exists in the outside world. The problem therefore, with the psychological reductionist, is that the "object" of contemplation is for him *nothing more than* the symbolization process from which it derives.[4]

In direct opposition to such a viewpoint as this it is my personal understanding that contemplative experience is not the imaginary and "visionary" sort of thing that many psychologists make it out to be. There is no question, of course, but that contemplative experience does involve a process of symbolization as a concrete way of representing the object of experience to oneself. On this point there exists a vast difference between an abstract and purely rational type of knowing and one that is closely bound up with images and symbols. What I would refuse to concede, however, is that contemplation is not a mode of knowing at all, as though the paradigm of all types of contemplative experience is that which associates itself with dreams, hallucinations, and visions. Actually it is a problem of careful inductive examination to determine in which instance the contemplative experience is genuine and authentic and in which instance the person in question is "carried away" by dreams, imaginations, and visions.

Barring the fact, of course, that many persons are often misled by their imaginations, the truth of the matter is this—that *contemplation is itself a mode of knowledge which*

4. To the reductionist, contemplation is nothing more than a kind of absorption in the **symbols** that one, consciously or otherwise, spins out of one's head. Accordingly, if you ask him whether these symbols have any "meaning" he will immediately respond that they do, **but** that their meaning is to be taken only with reference to the person who gives them their meaning, which is another way of saying that they have no real basis in fact. While it is granted therefore, in such a view, that an "objectification" process does take place and that the symbols of contemplative experience contain certain definite "referents" of their own, it is in no way admitted that contemplation is itself a mode of knowing, or better yet, of **understanding** something that is objectively and intimately **given** in experience.

in its concreteness and richness of meaning transcends any other mode. As I see it, the meaning of contemplation can be found only with reference to the object on which it is based: philosophic truth for the philosopher, beauty for the artist, and the love of God and man for the religious. The whole problem today with the reductionist is his total failure, in spite of all the talk about "symbolization," "objectification," etc., to understand that contemplation can and does have an object.

On this last point, although I am in many other respects in disagreement with the "objectivism" of Ayn Rand, I find myself in basic agreement with the general orientation of her philosophy. Not that Ayn Rand holds any brief for contemplation, but she does believe, and rightly so in my view, that there is an objective order of things to be accounted for, whether we will that order to exist or not. But back to the essential point: not only is it false to say that contemplative knowledge is an implicit form of illusion, but to the contrary, it relates more intimately to the objective order of things and persons than does any other mode of "practical" knowledge so-called.

Until now we have said much concerning pragmatism both as a philosophy and as a way of life. We have noted that pragmatism contains a profound element of truth in the stress that it places on the need for integration between philosophy and life. The weakness of pragmatism, however, lies not in what it asserts but in what it denies, namely, the quality of the human intelligence to penetrate to the very center of things. It is simply false to imagine that man creates his own truths, as though there were no objective order of reality to which his intelligence is, as Dewey rightly remarks, a "mode of response."

The basic shortcoming, however, of Dewey's philosophy,

and, for that matter, also of George Santayana's (1863-1952) is his failure to know that contemplation has anything more than a purely aesthetic value. To Dewey some men *need* contemplation, but let no one suppose that the object of their endeavor is anything more than the product of their own minds.

As against all these modes of philosophic thought that either distort or deny the authentic meaning of a contemplative approach to reality, let it be said that philosophy as wisdom has as one of its primary tasks that of at least pointing the way to the kind of interiorization we have already accounted for a few pages back. If at this stage of history it is capable of no other task, philosophy can at least enable modern man to recapture his sense of wonder concerning the world and himself and, in the bargain, remove those obstacles that have so long served as a barrier to the basic natural realism of the human mind. Unless man can become as a child again, the sophistication of modern society will cause him to collapse under the weight of a culture that no longer provides a pathway to the real. *Philosophy, then, should begin in wonder and end in enlightenment, even though all too often it begins in doubt and ends in a state of confusion.*

Concluding Remarks

The burden of this chapter has been to show that philosophy as integral realism is a method for helping to restore the balance between action and contemplation in the life of modern man. By integral realism I do not mean a bland kind of objectivism according to which one acknowledges that the world we observe with our senses is a world that really exists. This much is taken for granted. Rather integral realism is an attempt to explain, not merely the outer world as such, but the relationship that exists, or should exist, between the deep inner world of the human psyche and the world of outer experience. It is an attempt to circumvent the extremes of a naive realism, on the one hand, and a kind of introspectionism on the other, that restricts the individual to the categories of his own mind.

Yet beyond this the purpose of this chapter has been to show that integral realism is something more than philosophic theory. Our leading interest is to show its relevancy—*as therapy*—to the central problem of modern life, which is the lack of an authentic interiorization of the human spirit. The problem has been to show that the neuroses of modern life are largely the result of a failure to achieve this process of interiorization. As for the method of attaining it, we have suggested, in however inadequate a way, that there is a need for a balance between action and contemplation. Contemplation by itself can become sterile; action if it becomes one-sided, tends to become blind. The balance between action and contemplation can only be achieved by a living commitment to the inner world of experience as one which provides the kind of direction we need to give meaning to our "outer" lives. A long time ago a great philosopher, St. Thomas Aquinas, said that the measure of the meaning of an action is taken from the depth of the interior wellspring from which it arises. Those words were never truer than they are in our own day. The great need today is for an interiorization through silence and "humility before being" that can give depth and meaning to our lives.

One of the leading contentions of this book up to this point has been that philosophy as wisdom can play a vital role in re-orientating the life of modern man. One of the hidden premises of my argument is that the "role" of philosophy (if we may speak in those terms) is in part a social role. It is the object of the chapter that follows to explore the implications of that assumption.

12

▰▰▰▰▰▰▰▰▰▰▰▰▰▰▰▰▰▰▰▰▰▰▰▰▰▰▰▰▰▰▰▰▰▰▰▰▰

INTEGRAL
REALISM AND
THE
PHILOSO-
PHER'S SOCIAL
CONCERN

*Introductory
Remark*

As an opening
remark to one of his chapters on social and political philosophy, Schopenhauer declares it to be a characteristic failing
of the Germans to look in the clouds for what lies at their feet,
and well might this dictum serve as a reminder to all social
theorists, philosophers included, who lay claim to any insights into men and the affairs of men rather than into the
abstract realm of ideas as such. In fact, the problem with
most social theory today is its failure to respond to the
radical needs of human experience as such. In a sense it has
become too scientific in its self-conscious attempt to preserve a purity of method that is seldom in consonance with
such a basic fact as the ultimate reality of freedom.

But more of this later. At this point I simply want to
introduce the reader to the central aim of this chapter,
which is to show the need for some creative thinking on a
philosophical plane, in the area of social concern. The problem today is to reawaken philosophers from their anti-dog-

matic slumbers in the hope of getting them to respond to what has been and is to this day an integral part of their vocation. When philosophers again speak out in those areas of social concern that affect the life of society today, we may once more expect a sense of direction in society that will stimulate new vitality and growth.

The Need for Creative Thinking

Great philosophy, like great art, is the result not of a slavish imitation of other men's styles, but of an original attempt to develop one's personal insights into and relate them to, the ultimate nature of the real. One does not, of course, peer into the nature of the real as though it were a kind of magic glass or crystal ball. And it is vain to imagine that the pipe dreams of philosophers have any more efficacy than those of other men. But this is hardly the point. The point is to show that philosophers, of all men, have a special obligation to society at large—which is to provide for their fellowmen a sense of direction that is otherwise lacking in those whose work is so highly specialized that they seldom come up for air.

As I see it, the essential condition for *any* type of creative thinking in philosophy is that of "coming up for air" in the sense of achieving a certain kind of transcendence. In other words, one must achieve a certain transcendence over the values of a given society so as to be able to examine those values in a critical and highly objective light. All men are, of course, in varying degrees, children of their times, and it is sheer pretense to imagine that anyone can judge his own society in a totally objective light. Yet to suggest the contrary thesis that no one can be a judge in his own case is to assume that history and history alone is the judge.

Integral Realism and Social Concern

A New Approach to Social Philosophy

One of the most famous dicta of Karl Marx is his statement to the effect that philosophers before his time had only *theorized* about reality whereas the point of philosophy is to change it. Whether this statement is historically accurate or not, it contains a large measure of truth, especially regarding the split that has taken place between theory and practice. All too many philosophers have to this day withdrawn from the area of social concern into a purely specialized discipline of their own that is totally unrelated both to the problems of individual and social life. Others, however, like Dewey, have given serious attention to the relation between philosophy and life but failed to provide an adequate basis in theory for the facts they have attempted to interpret. In short, they have failed to get beyond purely pragmatic interpretations of values.[1] The position I am trying to develop in this book is to show that there can and should be *an integration not only between philosophy and life, but between values and facts, between theory and practice, between the area of individual concern and the facts of social life.* Such a philosophy I have called an "integral realism."

But let us try to get some insight into integral realism as it relates to social life by raising this fundamental question. Is man social only by way of convention and purely as a matter of pragmatic concern or of utilitarian interest? In the history of classical thought it is a long-standing tradition to maintain this somewhat arbitrary thesis. Such was the case,

1. For example, they have failed to see that there is a basis in human nature itself for some of the values, like democracy, which they rightly defend.

for example, with Rousseau and Hobbes, for both of whom man is essentially concerned with his individual interests and only secondarily with the interests of society at large. No need here, however, to go into a detailed analysis of all the social contract theories that have invaded the modern world except to remark that sociological positivism as we know it today is the contemporary counterpart of the classical modern theories of men like Hobbes, Rousseau, and Comte.

Let us here restate the question: *Is man by nature both social and political* or should we assume in positivistic fashion that it was only for reasons of convenience that he organized himself into social and political units from the time of the earliest civilization to our own day? Positivists no doubt will answer this question by referring to the fact that *all* social and political institutions are the result of a gradual development of the progress of the human race itself, and on this point I would readily concede that they are fundamentally right. There is no one institution—political, social, or domestic—that did not in some fashion and with a measure of trial and error evolve from the potentialities of its original status to the actualities of its later development. Such a statement, however, is beside the point. The point is to know that the development and growth of all such social institutions is rooted in the fundamental nature of the human race itself. No one will deny, of course, that men organize themselves into social and political societies for reasons of convenience and the like. *But the fundamental reason for their doing so is to serve the basic needs of the spirit.* This is to say that men, in addition to their external, physical, and biological needs, have to live in society in order to communicate with each other as persons and in order to share and develop their social, cultural, and religious needs

192

in the company of other men. Only the most superficial view of the nature of social reality can obscure our intelligences to the truth of this fundamental fact.

This much, however, for the origin of socio-political institutions as we know them today. These institutions, including such international societies as the U.N., are the combined result, if you will, of a certain "rational" instinct in man to unite in common purpose with his fellowmen and his attempt through trial and error to develop social institutions that will serve his fundamental goals, such as world peace.

Regarding the problem of "integral realism" and the area of social concern it is a question of knowing that man, within the context of his social and political milieu, acts according to the kind of being that he is, as one who, unlike anything else in nature, is both intelligent and free. At the present stage of discussion the reader may well suspect that my own view of "integral realism" is a simplistic revival in modern garb of the old Aristotelian social and political philosophy. And in a sense it is, but I trust, much more than that. While I readily acknowledge the element of truth both in Plato's and Aristotle's political theories, I feel that a modern interpretation of the meaning of society and its goals must be given in the light of the experience, not simply of the ancient Greeks, but of the world as we know it today.

What, then, is the most outstanding characteristic of integral realism as we begin to apply it in the social and political domain? This is no easy question to answer but I wish to state first of all that integral realism in contrast to any and all of the classical theories seeks to discover the balance in society between the two poles of structure and change. No doubt the central defect of all classical theories —what with all of the genuineness of their emphasis on the idea of a common good—is the excessive emphasis on structure and the minimal attention that was given to change. The intent of this remark is not, of course, to reproach Plato or Aristotle for a failure to appreciate the element of change, but merely to indicate that change is a feature that characterizes modern life in a way that is altogether unique. For this reason, too, any modern theory of social institutions and life must thoroughly account for change. Let us state, then, in unequivocal terms, that integral realism is no mere static conception of the nature of social reality, but to the contrary, one which takes fully into account the dynamism of change. More so than at any previous time change is, as it were, a built-in feature of modern life.

Along with this overall characteristic of a kind of universal change there is a second dominant characteristic of society as we know it today, and this is the desire for unity. In and through the profound changes that are taking place in society today men are striving toward what Josiah Royce referred to in his time as "the beloved community." Without becoming lyrical about it, the concept of the "beloved community" is one that involves the notion of men working with each other toward the fulfillment of common goals, such as the goal of racial equality as exemplified in the "freedom marches" of the early and mid-sixties.

Our philosophy of social reality would, however, be based on a pure illusion were we to imagine in utopian fashion that the present evolutionary state of mankind is one of unison and harmony. At the present stage of the history of mankind vast areas of the world are engaged in mortal combat with each other and the crisis between East and West, especially between China (even as a member of the U.N.) and the Western nations, will be long in the making before it is

194

finally resolved—and no one at this stage of history knows *how* it will be resolved.

It thus appears that the world as we know it today is one that is marked not only by a pluralism of political and social institutions (a basically healthy condition), but far less fortunately by a system of institutions that are at war with each other or within themselves. Yet given all this to be so, the author could hardly agree with the pessimism of Hobbes that the *natural* condition of mankind is one of perpetual warfare. There is nothing inevitable about war except for those who refuse to resolve world conflicts by any other means.

One of the essential theses therefore of integral realism in the area of social and political concern is the contention based on the evidence of certain facts that the evolutionary development of mankind in the economic sphere is moving toward an increased measure of socialization, whether in the countries that are controlled by communism or in those that are under the auspices of a democratic regime. This fact is, of course, of great significance for the future development of mankind. Men today are dependent upon one another in a measure they seldom were in the past—both as individuals and even as nations. Today entire nations, especially the smaller ones, are dependent not only on their own resources, but on the resources of other nations as well, both in the politico-economic and cultural sphere, for their future development.

One of the great problems today, of course, is that of *how* the larger nations are to provide the kind of assistance that the smaller nations need. The problem here is in part one of both motivation and method. If, for example, the motivation of a larger nation in providing assistance to, let us say, a newly emerging country, is merely to use that country in a struggle for world power and control, then no-body benefits in the end and the peace of the world becomes even more remote than it was before. However, even with good motivation a large nation can often bungle its way through foreign affairs by failing to consider the real needs of the smaller country, and most especially the need for an independence of spirit whereby the small nation can solve its own problems in its own way.

Enough has been said at least to indicate how an integral realism in the field of political philosophy would begin to approach the problem of world peace. As for the future, no one can look into it through a crystal ball. But all present indications are to the effect that in spite of world conflicts or perhaps even in a sense because of them, mankind seems to be moving in the direction of "one world"—a world which, it is hoped, will some day be in a position of relative peace, and in which some of the larger economic problems of the underdeveloped nations will have received the measure of attention they deserve.

But let us at this point abandon our conjecture as to the future. The point of this chapter is to show the need in the area of social concern for the development of a mature philosophy which as "integral realism" will take fully into account the ultimate realities—perhaps chief among them being man's constant and unremitting search for new and more creative goals—of human political and social life. Most important of all, the time has come for philosophers to devote all the energies of their intelligence toward promoting the evolutionary development of mankind—both materially and spiritually—in the direction of a fuller realization of itself.

Freedom and Order in Modern Life

As philosophy moves in the direction of a synthesis of

196

those dynamic factors that lie at the subconscious base of modern life, it must devote its attention to a reconciliation of the seemingly opposite poles of order and freedom. From the time of Plato to our own day men have thought of freedom and order in "either-or" terms, as though a choice must be made between one or the other of these values. As I see it, it is the work of integral realism to show that the only society that "makes sense" is the one that develops a system of laws and customs that reconcile these apparent antinomies. No doubt the ancient Greeks, Plato included, stressed order to the point that only the "citizens" and rulers were free. Everyone, so to speak, had to fit into a certain kind of "slot" and it had been assumed by Aristotle that there was a class of men who were "natural slaves."

Modern democratic theory is, of course, based on the assumption, both legitimate and true, that *all* men, from the standpoint of their natural rights, are born free. Nor is it assumed in a modern democracy that any given individual should on the basis of his present situation in society be confined to a "natural place." There may, of course, be considerable disadvantages to society if a rock singer becomes a governor or president, but the point is that democracy as we know it today acknowledges a certain mobility where by anyone with the right opportunity can emerge from his present situation or class. (No longer is it assumed or imagined that everyone must in purely Aristotelian fashion be placed into a given category or predicament.)

Interesting as it might be to develop at length a theory of democratic government, my only concern at the moment is to suggest that the balance of freedom *and* order is an essential condition for the growth of a society that is desirous of moving toward new goals. Accordingly, I beg to disagree with the opinion (held by some) that the "final end" or purpose of man is for him to be free. Freedom is indeed an all-important *condition* of human life but we should hardly identify this condition with a final goal. It would be equally wrong, of course, to say that *order*, or the element of structure in society, is its goal. The goal of society if we may so express it in very general terms is the happiness of men who move toward that goal, the conditions being freedom (with the equality of rights it supposes) and order (insofar as it involves a just and proper distribution of material and other types of goods).

What Is the Goal?

A moment ago I referred to "happiness" as the goal not only of individuals, but also of social and political life. "Happiness" is, of course, an elusive term because it fails to specify the object, end, or good in which happiness consists and, in any case, we must make a distinction between finite and proximate goals and those that are ultimate. In total agreement with the basic teleological character of Aristotle's ethics and political philosophy, I should wish to say that "happiness" on the level of man's *temporal* welfare as a citizen of the state and as a member of temporal society, lies in a proper distribution of those goods and even more fundamentally, of those *rights,* that are not only suited but necessary for a full human life.

No need at this point to spell out what all these goals and rights might be. It is enough rather to indicate that they include in their number the right to life, liberty, and the pursuit of happiness itself *together with* a sufficiency of those economic goods that are necessary to its actual attainment. Every man, for example, has the right to work for a living. But this is meaningless unless economic conditions are such that he can put it to use. More generally, the "pursuit of happiness" means little or nothing unless there is reasonable hope of its success or fulfillment.

Let no one imagine at this point, however, that the happiness of man consists in a vague and indeterminate kind of progress for its own sake. In the past we have seen enough of those utopian philosophies that have made a religion of progress as though each succeeding generation of men should sacrifice itself (in some slavish way) for a goal that only one generation in the end, namely the last, will enjoy. Such a goal, I say, is a pure chimera and for this reason it is important to know that the goal of life is not nor can it ultimately be either a finite temporal good nor a good or set of goods that is reserved only for a privileged elite.

The British utilitarians were on the right track when they stressed the point that happiness for mankind must be happiness for the greatest possible number of men. They were wrong, however, in thinking of this happiness chiefly or exclusively in quantitative or mathematical, rather than qualitative, terms. "Happiness" as an ultimate goal of life cannot be identified with any set of material goods, no matter how ideally they are distributed, since the end, goal, or purpose of human life, both individual and social, must finally be achieved on the level of transcendence—which is to say, on the level of the good of the spirit that will ultimately lead man to union with the Author and the End of his nature. A development of this consideration, however, would take us far beyond the scope of this book.

Let us therefore rest the matter at this point by saying that the goal of life, as visualized by an integral realism, is one which seeks a balance between temporal goods as such and those of the spirit. A superabundance of temporal goods with no reference to the goods of the spirit can only

lead as it so often has in the past to a condition of degeneration and decay. Exclusive emphasis, however, on the goods
of the spirit when the basic needs of the body are uncared
for, is not only irrelevant but futile. Just as it is wrong therefore to suppose that men can live without bread, so too is it
equally mistaken to think that bread alone will suffice.[2]

Rational and Subconscious Life: The Integration of the Two

When Plato wrote his *Republic* he felt that certain classes
of men like thieves, robbers, and perverts, should be exiled
from the company of their fellowmen. Modern society by
contrast has tended perhaps to take too soft-hearted and
permissive an attitude toward the criminal element within
society with the result that there is, on the surface at least,
a great deal more disorder than there was in Plato's time,
and the same holds true not only in regard to the criminal
element within society but to extremist groups of all sorts.

Be all this as it may, it is the work of integral realism as
social and political theory to see the need for achieving
a balance in society between its rational and irrational
"parts." What I am suggesting, of course, is the fact that the
pluralism of modern life gives rise to all sorts of elements in
society that are frequently antagonistic to the good order of
the state that acknowledges their rights. The problem that
naturally arises, then, is what to do with the dissenters.
Granting that criminals, once convicted by due process of
law, should be put behind bars, there are many others who
comprise that vociferous and sometimes too, that hidden,

2. Or what is worse, to think as Marie Antoinette, that cake could take
the place of bread.

minority which is regarded as the "lunatic fringe." So the problem is what to do with the lunatic fringe.

One sort of reaction, of course, is simply to deport the lunatic fringe in the confident hope that once society is purged of its extremist and irrational elements, it might then preserve itself in quiet dignity, order, and peace. Such, however, is a typically Platonic reaction to the antinomy between freedom and order, a reaction which solves the problem by "throwing out the baby with the bath." Unfortunately, however, this solution is based on a method which prescribes that the solution to problems generally consists in a total denial or disregard of one of their essential data.

As matters stand therefore the "data" of the problem of freedom and order are freedom *and* order, and this being so, one does not "solve" the problem by sacrificing one value at the total expense of the other but rather by making an attempt to secure a total integration of the two. *The making of just such an attempt—what with all of its imperfections and mistakes—is one of the great achievements of democracy as we know it today.* Scandalous as it may appear to outsiders, democracy in its modern form makes it quite possible for men of all sorts to live together if not in harmony and peace, at least with a juridical sense of the rights of those with whom they disagree. As it has often been said, politics is the art of the possible, and in no more profound sense is this dictum true than it is with reference to the accomodation that exists within a democracy between its rational and irrational "parts," between the twin sets of values of order and freedom.

Law as a principle of order is a restriction upon people's rights but only to the extent that the rights of other persons are in the process efficaciously fostered and maintained. Freedom, on the other hand, often makes it difficult for the law to take hold, but this is one of the risks involved in a democratic state and a permanent challenge to lawmakers to create laws that have the dual character of being enforceable and just. More importantly, however, what I am trying to say is this: better in a democracy to tolerate a measure of disorder, what Plato colorfully calls the "irrational" element in society, than completely to ban or suppress it. The subconscious, even on a social level, sooner or later will "have out," and it is a mark of a statesman to know how to "contain" this element, to keep it under surveillance, rather than to maintain an uncompromising position of absolute and rigid control. As I see it, one of the essential differences between democracy as a form of government and its opposed modern forms is the right of the individual and various groups within society to express in practical and effective terms the basis of their discontent. Just as in ordinary affairs it is important to allow people to have a "voice" in expressing their own point of view, so too in a democracy is it necessary to "hear out" the voice, however strident it may be at times, of those with whom we dissent.

Concluding Remarks

We have come a long way in the direction of showing how philosophy should respond—realistically and *integrally*—to the conflicts of modern life. Earlier in this volume I have stressed the notion of philosophy as therapy. I do not wish to abandon it here. Just as there are neuroses in the lives of individuals as such, so too in the life of society as a whole. We have the extreme phenomena of mass hysteria, riots, revolutions, and the like. It is a matter of simple observation to know that social life is also inflicted with milder neuroses of all sorts, and it is in part the work of the social and political philosophers to know how to treat not only the symptoms of these conflicts but their causes as well.

Further, the philosopher, insofar as his work extends beyond the sphere of helping to enlighten individuals as such, should also be a critic of and a participant in, the society in which he lives. As a critic he must develop a kind of shrewd instinct for smelling out whatever is meretricious or false in the exaggerations of those who can see no more than the part in lieu of the whole. *As a participant and as an integral member of the society to which he belongs, the philosopher must do all that he can as philosopher and citizen to make people conscious of their common goals.* Nor should anyone imagine that any sort of goal will do, but only those that harmonize with the freedom and dignity of man.

Finally, the philosopher as a true meta-psychologist, in the sense of one who goes beyond the symptoms to the cause, even in the order of social events, will take fully into account the reality of certain subconscious tendencies that demand full expression in a democratic state.[3] His own concern as a philosopher should be to do whatever lies in his power to direct these tendencies toward meaningful and lasting goals.

3. Conventionally, this is the sort of task that is reserved—sometimes in Machiavellian style—to politicians and rulers. My personal concern is that in a democracy we should not allow the rulers a greater freedom of hand than they need. In fact, it is precisely in those situations when intellectuals in general, and philosophers in particular, are silent, that the politicians, "smelling out" the vacuum that exists, begin to pre-empt for themselves powers that strictly lie outside of their own control. Here again it is not just a question of a philosopher king or nobody, but a question of making politicians susceptible to the advice of their grass-roots intellectual critics. The point here is that if philosophers are mute on the question of goals within our society, together with the means of achieving them, then their role will be pre-empted by other men who are often not equal to the task.

While it has been reserved therefore for our times to discover in full-blown fashion both the reality of human freedom and its necessity, it is the perennial work of the philosopher, especially in our times, to direct the *use* of that freedom toward the realization of *meaningful* goals. Such is the challenge of integral realism in the area of social concern.

13

TOWARD A
PHILOSOPHY
OF CULTURE

Introductory
Remarks

Back in the
nineteen-fifties Erich Fromm wrote a book entitled *The
Sane Society* with a view toward suggesting various ways,
from a societal point of view, in which human aspirations
might be more adequately fulfilled, or, as we might express
it today, he wrote with a view toward improving the *quality*
of human life. As the purpose of this book is not too widely
different from that which motivated the earlier work of
Fromm, I have attempted to provide the reader up to this
point with an outline of a new approach to philosophy that
will serve to relate its perennial goals to the more urgent
demands of society as we know it today. The present chapter
is a continuation of that same fundamental objective, but
with a particular emphasis on the development of a philosophy of culture as it specifically relates to the problems of
American life.

As we approach the 200th year of this nation's birth,
more and more people in this country are concerned, rightly
and radically so, with the development of some new ideas
that will carry us beyond the pragmatisms of the past. It is
enough for now to have made a beginning in the formation
of the fundamental values that have led to the growth of

this country, but that growth by and large has been a wild, unconscious thing often inspired with little more than the lust for life itself. What has been lacking is a sense of direction that might serve to control and guide the uninhibited desire (as under President Polk in the eighteen forties) for territorial and imperialistic expansion. Today people are wondering why this nation should feature itself, however benignly so, as the Number One Policeman-of-the-World, and they are beginning to wonder if there is not a more fundamental need for domestic reform in the way of a radical re-thinking of the goals of our national life.

The aim of this chapter is to show that one of the prime ingredients for the development of this sense of goals is a correlative understanding of the need for a philosophy of culture. Ultimately, only two alternatives lie open to modern man: either he can drift unreflectively with the tide of an uninformed public opinion and thus become the victim of every passing fad or experiment or he can begin to use his God-given freedom and intelligence to assert his essential dignity as a man. The pursuit of this latter alternative carries with it the seeds of a new future that can—against all odds—provide a new path in which the essentially qualitative feature of human life will be restored.

Philosophy and Culture

At a moment in human history, when so to speak, the house is burning down, there is little time or occasion for the making of hair-splitting distinctions of the sort that philosophers have indulged in for the past three or four hundred years. What we need today rather is a radical re-thinking of the goal and purpose of philosophy itself in a way that is "relevant" (if I may use a much-overworked expression) to the ends and purposes of human life. Philosophy indeed has a speculative value which I would be the last to deny, but its speculative value derives, not from any sterile analysis that preoccupies itself with pseudo-mind-body problems or, if you will, the problems of "other minds," but from a vital and dynamic contact with the existential real, especially as it relates to the so-called "problem of man."

Yet to speak of the "problem of man" is to toy with an ambiguous phrase, since man far from being a mere "problem," is a mystery both to himself and to his fellow men. When I speak of the mystery of the human person I mean that there are depths of longing, aspiration, love, hate, and of all the other emotions in the human psyche that far transcend any and all of the methods either of the physical or of the social sciences. Further, it is these depths of inner awareness and sub-conscious motivation that present a perennial challenge both to the philosopher and to the theologian for an increased understanding of the nature of man, whether we regard him as an individual person or as a member of a living and ongoing social unit—be that unit as small as the family or as large as the nation itself.

The point as to the *mystery* of the human person is one that bears emphasis in this day and age especially in view of the futile attempts on the part of earlier philosophers like Hume to construct what they regard as a "science" of human nature which, once properly developed, would presumably hold the key to a millennium of future growth and happiness. Briefly, let us get a bird's-eye view of some of these conflicting philosophies of human culture and progress, especially as conceived by such notables as Hegel, Comte, Marx, and Nietzsche.

207

Each of these figures (and many others besides) had a dream in *their* time for the future of the human race. Hegel's dream—in the wake of the eighteenth century Enlightenment—was that of the rule of Reason in which someday man through his consciousness and freedom would be *aufgehoben* (that is, "taken up," transformed," "synthesized") in the womb of an Absolute State. As for Comte, he too, like Hegel, saw human history in various stages of development. Yet, *unlike* Hegel, Comte had a dream in which theological and metaphysical myth (so-regarded) would soon give way to the new era of the positive sciences. Science and science alone could prepare the way for the new religion of humanity in which man himself would become the object of his own ceremonial worship. Thirdly, as most of our contemporaries know, Marx hatched a dream of his own in the dusty halls of the British Museum—the dream of the rule, not of reason, nor of scientific man as Comte had conceived him, but of the proletariat. Some day all men would in fact be equal—even though George Orwell will remark (a few generations later) in his *Animal Farm*—that some will be *more* equal than others. As for Nietzsche, he was too much of an aristocrat to accept the dream of a universal working class. Nietzsche's dream would culminate rather in the will-to-power and the rule of the *Ubermensch*. Thus spake Zarathustra.

This much, however, for the 19th century, for what we want to know now is something about our own lives and times. In an earlier chapter, I had already referred in a favorable light to the dream of Josiah Royce of a Beloved Community in which loyalty to the human race would serve as the order of the day. That dream, however, was shattered by the onslaught of World War I only to be revived in a new form by none less than the President of the United

208

States. Though not a professional philosopher, President Wilson went to the League of Nations in the hope of enacting a treaty that would for all time to come "make the world safe for democracy." Since that time we have come to know that neither the world nor democracy was safe and that democracy too, like national socialism and communism, can be used—often unwittingly—in the fashion of a knight-in-shining-armor to serve totalitarian ends.

Given the disillusionment of World War II it became popular for a time to reject all dreams. Witness, for example, *The Stranger* of Albert Camus and the radical pessimism in the *No Exit* of Jean-Paul Sartre. Given the condition of man as it is, hell *is* other people and life really has no meaning. Here we find Sartre in essential agreement with Schopenhauer on the point that all we can do is to alleviate our misery by temporary methods of escape. Each man must create his own project, and never again must man entertain the illusion that there can be a single project for the whole of mankind.

This, then, was the mood that prevailed especially in some parts of Europe in the aftermath of World War II, but happily the mood of despair would soon give rise again to the beginnings of a new philosophy of hope. As a direct counter-agent to the Sartrean themes of anxiety, nausea, and despair, we find men like Gabriel Marcel helping to revive the hope that springs eternal in the human breast, and there are signs on the horizon (thanks to some young German theologians) that hope will soon be the "in" thing again.

However, it is not the business of philosophers to follow fads even if against their best intentions they sometimes create them, and for this reason I want to revert to the challenge that faces philosophers today. This challenge is quite simply that of facing up to the "problem of man" (so-called) not insofar as man is a problem to be solved by some quasi-mathematical or scientific means, that is, in the direction of a new "science of human nature," but an intelligible mystery who in the inner depths of his being is searching for truth and for happiness even more so than he is searching for bread and wine. It has often been said that it belongs to the wise man to place things in order ("sapientis est ordinare"), but how is it possible to know *how* to order and direct unless the wise man in question has some teleological hint of the direction in which man—in the present state and condition of society—can and should move? The challenge that exists for philosophers is that of articulating in the clearest way possible—and in the light of all of the wisdom of the past—which *are* which are *not* the real needs of modern man and wherein lies the answer to those needs. A thousand times and again it has been said that salvation does not lie in technology alone, and most persons in their better moments know this to be so. But beyond this it is the business of the philosopher to relate the use of technology—as an integral part of modern culture—to significant human goals.

The reason I must emphasize this point is rooted in the fact that science does not have the answer to the questions which modern man asks himself, and on this point I quote Jacques Maritain:

"Medicine can recommend sobriety, psychology can recommend humility, and even, if need be, religious faith as detergents and lubricants for our human springs . . . but what answer can they give when they ask themselves, for example, whether trial marriage, euthanasia, and scientifically controlled abortion or biochemical manip-

210

ulation of the nerve centers are to be recommended or advised against . . . whether for a nation at war it is a crime or a duty to insure victory by using a weapon which annihilates millions of people . . . ?"[1]

Let us grant, then, that although modern science and modern technology have become, not only an integral, but a dominant element in the shaping of modern society and culture, neither science nor technology hold the key to the basic dilemmas that society is faced with today. None of these dilemmas, of course, will be resolved by consulting some kind of modern counterpart of the Oracle of Delphi as it would be hoping for too much to suppose that any one man or group of men, no matter how wise, would hold the riddle of the sphinx. Yet in any event the dilemmas of modern life are something more than a riddle just as man himself is something more than a problem, and futile as it is to look for panaceas, the situation of modern man can only deteriorate until and unless some kind of wisdom tradition is revived and restored. A society and a culture that is totally lacking in a wisdom tradition of its own, that is, of the sort which would give that society an inner impulse toward creativity and inner spiritual longing, toward even a secular kind of holiness, will ultimately go the way of all the other civilizations (so elaborately traced out by Toynbee) that have perished from within.

Apropos, then, of the relationship between philosophy and culture, it should be noted that one of the prime defects of American culture, as this author sees it, is the spirit of cultural relativism that pervades the American scene—a relativism that can only be worsened if the philosophers

1. J. Maritain, **Moral Philosophy** (New York: Charles Scribner's Sons, 1964), p. 414.

8

themselves take a totally detached point of view to the question of values. Moral values are inextricably bound up with the cultural complex, and the failure to perceive that there are some things of permanent worth in any society can only lead to a condition not only of moral bankruptcy, but of a cultural anarchy in which anything goes. Accordingly, while cultural diversity (whether within a given society or nation or as something that marks one society off from another) is one of the more attractive features of the human race, cultural pluralism carried to the point of anarchy can only lead to confusion and decay. No society is any greater than the principle of unity that binds into a spiritual and moral whole elements that are otherwise diverse.

The Meaning of Culture and "The American Way of Life"

As we continue our analysis of various aspects of American culture and the stance that philosophers should maintain in regard to it, I want to give added precision to what I have in mind when I speak of "culture" in the first place, a word that need not be as elusive as it often appears to be. Every society is characterized by a predominant set of values—good, bad, or indifferent—which constitutes its basic milieu, and it is this idea of a shared community of values and traditions—whether they are deliberately planned and fostered or only subconsciously sustained, that comes fairly close to what I understand by "culture." Thus in the sense I use the term, "culture" may be taken to include something as profound as the monastic culture of the middle ages or as superficial as contemporary styles of living and of dress. In any event it is the predominant set of motivations and values as visibly displayed through some kind of outer expression that is the originating source of a "culture" of whatever sort. Too, it is the "culture" or set of "sub-cultures" that mark off the point of difference between one society and another.[2]

On the basis of this general idea of culture as a shared set of values that are operative within the larger community, a few comments are in order as to some of the dominant features of American culture as we know it today. No doubt the very magnitude and cultural diversity of this nation makes any generalizations as to a single culture hazardous, and the fact of the matter is that American society is a polyglot complex of a variety of cultures and sub-cultures. Even so, it is no mere product of abstraction to suggest that there *are* dominant features, some of them good, others bad, that do characterize the *modus vivendi* that is commonly referred to as "the American way of life."

Among these features is a certain kind of restlessness of the spirit which has both its good points and its bad. The inner restlessness of the American temperament has on the negative side led to a failure to appreciate and cultivate the values of silence and contemplation as we have traced out those values in Chapter 11—with the result that our society as a mass society is characterized by a certain type of neuroticism, not to be found, at least to the same degree, let us

2. The above description is in basic agreement with the following which is enunciated by Christopher Dawson: "When I speak of culture I am not thinking of the cultivation of the individual mind, which was the usual sense of the word in the past, but of a common social way of life—a life with a tradition behind it, which has embodied itself in institutions and which involves moral standards and principles. Every historic society has such a culture from the lowest tribe of savages to the most complex forms of civilized life. And every society can lose its culture either completely or partially, if it is exposed to violent or far-reaching changes." C. Dawson, **The Historic Reality of Christian Culture** (New York: Harper and Row Publishers, 1965), p. 13.

say, in other nations, as in Mexico and the Latin American countries, where a certain type of leisure is the order of the day. Too, it is a very easy temptation for a native American to condemn this attitude of mañana as a kind of laziness, a built-in sense of inefficiency that can only lead to starvation in the midst of an ever-exploding population that has gotten out of rational control.

Whatever the objective merits of this type of judgment, it is more often than not based on a failure to understand the positive qualities of cultures and societies other than our own and a tendency to superimpose our own remedies as panaceas for the deficiencies of the "underprivileged" nations. Yet a minimum of reflection will lead us to some realization of the fact that there exists in these other nations a richness of spiritual and religious traditions that belie their economic poverty, and from this point of view alone Americans have much to learn.

As to the positive side of "the American way of life"—if we may focus on its technological aspect—it is an undeniable fact that the fruits of technology have provided for the "average" American a higher standard of living than has generally been enjoyed by any other country in the history of the world. Medical technology has made rapid strides in the alleviation of human misery and in the saving of human lives; the erection of a vast educational system has made available to untold millions of Americans the resources of world culture and history of which they have largely been ignorant in the past; new methods of travel, especially in the form of jet transportation, have made it possible for millions of Americans each year to visit relatives and friends in the most remote parts of the country or of the world in a matter of hours; television has brought with it a form of instant communications in the areas of sports, politics, education, and world development that was undreamt of by our fore-fathers; and the conveniences of the American home, from air conditioning to the use of electric knives have taken much of the tedium out of human life. These benefits, I say, may (except in those cases where the use is purely frivolous) be counted among the assets of modern American life, but the very listing of these benefits suggests in one and the same breath the fact of their unequal distribution, as there continues to exist in this country a very large segment of the population, the forgotten poor, that suffers poverty in the midst of inflation and which has very little chance—even in the last part of the twentieth century—to improve its lot.

Yet the unequal distribution of wealth is only one aspect of the failure to achieve the "American dream." The other side of the coin is the fact that the misuse of goods—especially in those circles where they are enjoyed in super-abundance —has led "homo Americanus" into a condition of spiritual poverty that has made him unworthy, for all his heroics, of the benefits he has received. In fact, it is generally true that a too great abundance of wealth can lead, as indeed it has in this country, not only to a profligate waste of material resources together with all the forms of pollution (such as water and air pollution), but to a state of moral degeneracy as well. Side by side with the desire to *save* human life—at whatever cost or inconvenience—there has grown up in this country a more than seeming spirit of wastefulness in the sacrifice of human lives on the battlefields of remote countries where dubious wars are being fought and perpetuated. Too, for all the emphasis that has been traditionally placed on man's right to pursue freedom and happiness, we have allowed to develop in this country a system of organized and unorganized crime that makes life, especially in the large cities, a very hazardous affair. Crime in recent years has run rampant and there is no segment of the American population that has been exempt, if only from an economic point of view, from the tentacles of the criminal elements in our society, so much so that it is no exaggeration to speak of the growth of a "crime culture" that almost takes in stride, for example, the murder of innocent persons in the streets by teen-age and other types of gangs.

However, it is not my intent to draw up an indictment of failures. My only desire is to show a realistic concern for a deeper level of awareness of the seamier elements of the "American dream"—lest anyone who is romantically inclined be led into a state of illusion. No doubt Platonism as a philosophy or as a philosophic frame of mind has much to commend to one who is interested in culture. But if Platonism to the modern student of culture means nothing more than viewing the archetypes or exemplars of an ideal society, then it becomes quite easy to confuse, as many Americans do today, the ideal with the reality. A genuine philosophy of culture as it relates to the American scene must provide a sense of balance between the ideal as it is envisioned in symbols like the flag and the application of that ideal to the ongoing affairs of the everyday life of the nation.

The Positive Contributions of Philosophers

Nor do I wish my reader to imagine that I am indulging in a perverse kind of pessimism that sees only the negative side of the ledger, as it is my deepest conviction that there lies imbedded in the subsoil of the American character a deposit of good sense and judgment that will hopefully—against all forms of extremism—come to the fore. In the meantime, however, every effort should be bent not to trust to luck or to chance, but to "cup the flame" of those elements

216

within our society that can and do have a redemptive value for the good of the whole. The real problem, then, in the face of all the vulgarizing tendencies of a mass culture that has compromised its soul for the material goods of life is that of accepting and sustaining the challenge to reinforce those values that harmonize both with the dignity of man and the dignity of his calling to serve a reality higher than himself. The cheap, the tawdry, the vulgar must be replaced in all segments of American life with a sense of refinement, of delicacy, and of fundamental respect on all sides for other persons' rights. To this end it is hardly the vocation of the philosopher to pronounce an attitude of indifference to the values of society as though his only interest were in the "facts." Rather, philosophers, at least some of them, should regard themselves (in the phrase of Jacques Maritain) as a "prophetic shock minority" for sustaining the quality of human life, not only in terms of the physical, but also of the moral and spiritual environment, in the hope that at least the very *concept* of a public morality might be restored. Truly, then, has the order of wisdom been betrayed whenever the purveyors of sexual perversion, the advocates of violence, the criminal elements, and so on, seek to undermine the very foundations of society—without a word of protest from the philosophers. Of all men, philosophers (and theologians as well) have a civic and professional responsibility to give witness to the better elements within a culture in the hope of making these elements prevail against all handicaps and odds.

What needs to be stressed therefore within the context both of the American scene and of Western civilization at large are the elements of positive contribution in all of the great philosophers, whether one otherwise agrees with those philosophers or not. Thus Kant's great and central insight, for all of my criticism of his noetics in the earlier part of this book, was his humanitarian conception of men conceived as ends in themselves, not as means for anyone's sense of pleasure, power, or wealth—an insight that has a profound relevance to a society that is enmeshed in the spirit of pragmatism. Likewise, for another example, does Schopenhauer's idea of "Mitleid" ("sym-pathy") as a leading ethical motive relate to the need in our society today to achieve a measure (as I have spoken of it in an earlier chapter) of self-transcendence through love. Too, American society today is badly in need of understanding the key concept of Marx, according to which man is viewed as being "alienated from his work," in the hope that through this concept the dignity of human labor might be restored. Finally, and most important of all, American society is in dire need of the witness of Maritain's philosophy, which stresses the importance of achieving in all levels of society an "integral humanism"[3] that is subservient to the common good. Thus a true humanism is based on the idea of the intrinsic importance of every member of the body politic, on the idea that every member is a potential contributor to its health and well-being, on the conviction that the things which unite men in their common endeavors can be stronger than those which set them apart. Should such key concepts as these (and perhaps others more creative yet) be put to use, it is quite possible that the good will and common sense of the American public might ultimately prevail against a near pathological concern with uncontrolled experiments of all sorts.

3. J. Maritain, **Integral Humanism,** trans. by J. Evans (New York: Charles Scribner's Sons, 1968). This is one of the most rewarding books of modern times. Originally published as a French edition under the title of **Humanisme Intégral,** this new translation is a faithful rendition of the author's thought and ideas.

Toward A Philosophy of Culture

The Quantification of Meaning and the Need for Interior Growth

The brunt of the foregoing remarks has been to show the need in American society for the dynamics of the spiritual pre-conscious and the need as well for a creative minority in all areas of public life to give a new sense of direction to the impetus of American life. Too, *in view of the tendency toward extremism within the American cultural scene, there exists the need, not only for a balanced philosophy (which is lacking) but for a philosophy of balance that might help us to avoid the extremes,* especially in regard to the use of a technology that has not been critically evaluated in relation to the ends of human life. To sum up, the American tendency to romanticize, while well-motivated and good in itself, can through its lack of realism lead to dangerous extremes. The real need therefore carries us beyond the area of good intentions into the area of wisdom of life, and it was Cardinal Newman who once remarked that *no greater calamity can come to a good cause than that the wrong persons, however well motivated, attach themselves to it.* "Good causes" (of which there are plenty in America) are not enough: what is needed most of all is the presence of wise men who can determine whether these causes (like those which promote abortion and euthanasia) are really good, or whether they work to the detriment of man. Ignorance, indeed, has its depths even as does knowledge and wisdom, and unless the wisdom of the wise man prevails society will be worse off in the bargain.

Until now we have stressed the idea that it is in the awareness of meaningful goals that the real progress of society takes place just as it is the failure to conceive the right goals that leads to a state of decline. As regards the American scene there is one last defect to which I here call attention before I pass on to the "need for interior growth." This defect lies in a misconceived approach to the virtue of "magnanimity." Magnanimity *as a virtue* means the habit of doing great things for mankind. What this implies is a certain "greatness of soul" that conceives of doing great things, if need be, on a grand scale. Suppose, then, that we accept this definition. We should then have to admit that many aspects of American culture (like the exportation of vast quantities of goods to countries that are plagued with earthquakes, fires, or floods) are authentic expressions on a societal level of the virtue of magnanimity. Yet the authentic is quite often the exception rather than the rule, as the desire for greatness in this country is often confused with what social scientists sometimes call "the quantification of meaning." I am not quite sure what this oft-used expression signifies, but of one thing I am sure: even the British utilitarians for all of their emphasis on the greatest happiness for the greatest number of citizens would be reluctant to identify this happiness with the accumulation of material goods for their own sake, so that even to them the qualitative dimension of life in the body politic had a real and not a merely imaginary significance.

Yet such is not generally the case in this country. Greatness more often than not is thought of in quantitative terms and that with reference to the production of material goods, even in some cases, whether those goods are significantly usable or not. The cultivation of the arts, intellectual values, rational discussion and debate, the promotion of religion and morality—values of this sort are too often subordinated to the value that is placed on the "quantification of meaning" in terms of material goods alone. On this point no sharper critic can be found than the philosopher George Santayana. Speaking of the failure in American life to enjoy even sensible goods themselves, Santayana remarks:

> "The circumstances of his life . . . have necessarily driven
> the American into moral materialism; for in his dealings
> with material things he can hardly stop to enjoy their
> sensible aspects . . . . He is practical as against the poet
> and worldly as against the clear philosopher or the saint.
> The most striking expression of this materialism is usually
> supposed to be his love for the almighty dollar; but that
> is a foreign and unintelligent view. The American talks
> about money, because that is the symbol and measure he
> has at hand for success, intelligence, and power; but as to
> money itself he makes, loses, spends, and gives it away
> with a very light heart. To my mind the most striking ex-
> pression of his materialism is his singular occupation with
> quantity."[4]

As for the remedy of the defect which Santayana so
strikingly depicts in the quotation above, I would suggest, in
accordance with the central hypothesis of Chapter 11, that
the single most important habit of mind to cultivate is that

4. G. Santayana, **Character and Opinion in the United States** (New
York: W.W. Norton & Co., Inc., 1967), passim 187-189. In the same passage
Santayana continues to provide us with examples from his personal experience as follows: "If, for example, you visit Niagara Falls, you may expect
to hear how many cubic feet or metric tons of water are precipitated per
second over the cataract . . . Nor is this insistence on quantity confined to
men of business. The President of Harvard College . . . inquired how my
classes were getting on; and when I replied that I thought they were getting
on well, that my men seemed to be keen and intelligent, he stopped me
as if I was about to waste his time. 'I meant,' said he, 'what is **the number**
of students in your classes?'." Santayana concludes this remarkable
quotation as follows: ". . . To be poor in order to be simple, to produce
less in order that the product may be more choice and beautiful, and may
leave us less burdened with unnecessary duties and useless possessions—
that is an ideal not articulated in the American mind." **Idem.**

of the *interiorization* of life and culture. Ultimately, any culture, if it is to be authentic and harmonious with respect to the overall aims of human life must be based on an interior and reflective understanding of what is primary and what is not. Thus, for example, the great wealth of Texas is no compensation for the cultivation of letters and the arts, even though in many instances it is thought that good art, good literature, good philosophy, or what have you, could be imported like any other commodity on the market. Unfortunately, the goods of the spirit—to be truly significant— must be cultivated from within the individual and the society in which they are to reside, and the failure to do this will result in nothing more than what Toynbee calls the "mechanicalness of mimesis," and an imitation culture (like a second rate reproduction) is no culture at all. Ultimately, all true culture and all true art (however primordial the form) must be a reflection of the inward soul of the man and of the society in which they reside.

Concluding Remarks

In the face of the immaturity and adolescence of our American culture philosophers should be taking positive steps (so it would seem to me) toward an "integral realism" in philosophy—a realism which is integrated with the issues of the society in which we live. The problem, as I see it, is that the typically American mode of response to problems (both foreign and domestic) is based on a failure to know ourselves, our aims and our ambitions. Although we Americans continually parrot the language of freedom, opportunity, personal dignity, and the like, we seldom take time out to examine in depth the deeper spiritual implications of these terms. More precisely, we seem more concerned, relative to a new era of leisure, with multiplying experiences *on a horizontal plane* (on the level of "the quantification of meaning") than we are with developing them vertically and in depth. One of the challenges of the philosopher, then, is to re-interpret modern life in the light of the wisdom that is properly his domain, and by wisdom here I mean in particular practical wisdom, and that is only another name for prudence. Nor should we forget the point of what we said in Chapter 6 that military, political, or business prudence mean nothing and, as a matter of fact, can and do degenerate into the vice of cunning unless they are directed toward authentically human goals. As to the question of intemperance, especially in the realm of ideas, a certain type of moderation is a particularly desirable quality for Americans to learn to possess. I am not saying, of course, that we should be moderate in our legitimate and necessary demands for such matters as civil rights, but on the contrary, that we should press on until truly we have overcome. However, it is a typically American failure—in line with our puritan tradition—to repress our conflicts till the emergence of that dramatic moment when they have erupted into violent extremes.

No doubt philosophers (like everyone else) have their dreams, and I confess that one of my personal dreams is for a vibrant philosophy that is rooted in a realistic metaphysics, but which is also social and political in its orientation—a philosophy that will stand on its own feet against any attempt to rule it out of court. What we need in America today is a philosophy that will counteract, not the computer, but the computer mentality and help restore man as the inventor of the machines he has created and not the other way around.

EPILOGUE

THE
CHALLENGE
TO
PHILOSOPHY
TODAY

ENOUGH HAS BEEN
said in the course of these chapters to lead the reader into a
consciousness of the practical importance of philosophy for
our times. What I have said of the need for a reconstruction
in philosophy is only a prelude to the work that remains to be
done. In any case, it has not been the aim of this book to
have fully accomplished that task—but only in some concrete sense to have pointed out the way.[1]

What is important, however, is for the reader to get a
sense of perspective of the central themes of this work,
which may be recapitulated as follows. Modern man has,
under the impact of a long-standing subjectivism, lost
confidence in his capacity for a knowledge of objective truth.
The philosophers themselves have contributed to this state
of affairs by their own failure—along epistemological lines—
to establish a bridge as an efficacious point of contact between mind and reality. Too, this failure to establish contact

1. Happily there are hopeful signs on the horizon that philosophy in
this country is beginning to take a new turn as evidenced by the appearance of new courses in the philosophy curricula of our schools that are
dealing with the more concrete problems of social-political philosophy
and the publication of new journals like **Philosophy and Public Affairs**
(Princeton, N.J.: The Princeton University Press).

224

with the real world bespeaks the need of a reconstruction in philosophy of the sort that can take place only by penetrating beyond the surface level of rational, human consciousness to the inner needs of the spirit that lies within. Here in the depths of the psyche will it be found that there is no greater well-spring of a typically human behavior than the will-to-meaning and the desire for self-transcendence. Man is more than anything else a teleological being or creature whose end, purpose, or fulfillment lies outside of himself.

This being so, it is incumbent upon modern man—in this process of a true re-discovery of himself—to acknowledge and provide not only for the superficial needs of an oversold and exaggerated culture of the body, but for the profound and lasting needs of the spirit. What is needed here is a kind of therapy of the spirit that is based on an awareness of the hidden realities that lie within. Nor is it enough that these profound needs of the spirit be recognized only on the isolated level of a few individual consciences as such. Society itself must recognize these needs and look toward their fulfillment as an ideal, as a goal to be accomplished. Indeed, one of the reasons for the present sense of drift and aimlessness within our western society is its failure in the practical order to recognize the needs of the spirit.[2] In the place of a dedication to a transcendent set of ideals we have witnessed the triumph of pragmatism in our times—pragmatism in individual conduct, pragmatism in the professions, in government, in education, in domestic and foreign affairs.

This spirit of pragmatism has unhappily blunted the

---

2. For a long time it seems that western civilization has lived off the capital of its past Christian heritage, but this is no longer the case.

edge of our national conscience and given rise to a spirit of cultural relativism in which it is claimed that *all* values are relative to the society that creates them. Such a philosophy of politics and culture is based on a near total ignorance of man and the natural law which is an integral part of his very existence. Pragmatism, cultural relativism, subjectivism, (call this modern syndrome by whatever philosophical name you choose), has undermined respect for authority, freedom of self-determination, and a code of ethics that is universally binding on all men who have the capacity to understand it.

In the paragraphs above I have tried to compress for the reader the basic orientation of this work. However, as we reach toward some of its conclusions we must now explain, however briefly, the problem of philosophy and the future of man. Perhaps our main question is this: What *is* the future of man, or should we ask, even more radically, whether man shall have a future at all? No doubt there are enough congenital pessimists in the world to defend this latter hypothesis, and in view of the decline of morals in our society one might readily concede that they have a point. Too, some philosophers have spoken in somewhat guarded terms of "the death of man," as though it were an accomplished fact. For myself, I should like to take a more optimistic view. Man is no more dead than God can be said to be dead, depending, however, on the faith or the absence of it that lies within.

If man has ultimately and permanently lost confidence in himself, then no one in the world can persuade him of his chances of recovery, for the simple reason that human hope is both the necessary condition and indispensable wellspring of a new and as yet unsuspected life. But here lies the question: Is it still possible for modern man to recapture in his vision of the future the glorious image of himself as a

226

kind of "fallen god"? I do not mean to suggest that we all become neo-pythagoreans of sorts, but only that we have been looking on the dark side of human nature for so long, the side of anxiety and despair, that we have lost all cognizance of the hidden resources of energy, life and hope.

The question, then, as to whether man *has* a future, and that also of the *kind* of future he will have, is largely a question of hope, but a hope with a foundation in fact. The objective foundation of this hope is the realization that man cannot ultimately shift for himself, but that he depends ultimately upon the Providential Plan of a Being whom most men refer to as "God." In the long run only true humanism, in terms of one that provides an ultimate solution to the problem of life, is an integral humanism of the sort in which the ends of man are ultimately integrated with the ends, not of an arbitrary tyrant God, but of a beneficent Creator and Redeemer whose only concern is the good of man himself.

All of this talk about God, however, would be mere pious prattle were it not for the fact that man, left to his own resources, can do no more than organize the earth, the forces of technology included, against himself.[3] *Quare fremuerunt gentes et populi meditati sunt inania?*—"Why have the nations raged and why have the people meditated on vain things?" (Psalm 2). The complaint of the psalmist has much relevance to the crisis of our times and it calls our attention to the sad state of affairs in which man sees in the earth nothing more than the mirror of his own creations. In a very profound and frightening sense the return to a sane society can only be initiated and accomplished by a decisive

3. On this point see especially the Preface and Part One of Henri de Lubac, **The Drama of Atheistic Humanism** (New York: The World Publishing Co., 1969), trans. by E. M. Riley.

and efficacious return to the living God.

However, I do not mean to exaggerate the theological dimension of the problem of modern man, as the problem is also one of an ethical nature. Unfortunately, however, when most people think of ethics they think of it only on a superficial plane—on the plane of "good conduct" that is conformed in some slavish way to an external law. Yet on a much deeper level the ethical dimension of human existence implies a profound inner respect, a deep-seated sense of justice that extends to *all* men *as* men.[4] To regard men thus as men and from an inner conviction that emerges from the depths of the soul is to rise above the minimum dictates of the law, and it is on *this* level of morality that we can, in significant terms, talk and think about the future of man.

There resides in the depths of society a certain hidden element of goodness that needs to be tapped, and any attempt merely to coerce men into conformity to law ignores this fundamental fact. To illustrate my point: the problem of race relations in this country can never be solved on the level of law alone. Only for a limited time can the restraining force of the law quell riots and put racial wars to rest. The real need in this as in all other areas of human concern is, along with a sense of the dignity of man and his basic human rights, the cultivation of a quasi-mystical sense of the unity of man.

The future of man, then, lies ultimately in a kind of

4. Here it is interesting to note some of Hegel's remarks concerning the philosophy of civilization. According to him the original condition of mankind, as manifested in the earlier and more primitive forms of civilization, was such that the dignity of man was in no way recognized. However as civilization grew and developed there were some societies, notably that of ancient Greece, that recognized the dignity of some men. Yet, in Hegel's view, it was not until the coming of Christianity that the dignity of all men as men had been brought to the fore.

therapy and purgation of the spirit that will enable all men—ultimately in the midst of crisis—to see that their own welfare and happiness is intimately bound up with the happiness and welfare of other men. Leisure, automation, technology, or what have you, are only means, albeit very important means, for securing the desideratum of a human race that could some day (*relatively* speaking) be at peace with itself. But nothing less than a rejuvenation of the spiritual resources that lie within can ever accomplish the task. In the end what really matters is for man to know that the work of human redemption is an ongoing task which requires cooperation between God and man and between all men among themselves whether they believe in God or not. It is only in such a persevering effort that the future of man will be assured.

As for the task of philosophy, little need be said beyond what we have already said in this book. Philosophy does stand in need of reconstruction and reform, but along the lines, not of another knowledge explosion, but of an understanding in depth of the deeper meanings, conflicts, issues, and goals of human life. The great need, as we have repeatedly pointed out, is the need for a return to philosophy as wisdom. Finally, as to the accomplishment of this task, I would like to suggest that it begin in the schools, but if there is no chance of reform in those quarters, then let it begin where it may, and in the intelligence of anyone—be he an academic philosopher or not—who is up to the task. My own personal formation and development has taken place in the schools, but I have never believed that philosophy should be confined to the classroom alone. The challenge exists, then, for anyone properly qualified and inspired to meet it, and the purpose of this book has been well served if, in the end, some few individuals have been motivated in the reading of it to assume a role of intellectual leadership in the meeting of that challenge. Where there is no challenge, neither is there a response,[5] and one of the greatest challenges in this country is the re-alignment of the human intelligence in those matters of the human spirit that have the greatest consequences for human life.

5. Here I refer the reader to Arnold Toynbee's philosophy of challenge and response as outlined in various parts of his famous **A Study of History.** For a condensed version of the first six volumes of this monumental work see A. Toynbee, **A Study of History,** abridged by D. C. Somervell (New York: Oxford University Press, 1947).

Bibliography

Note:
The articles and books below in some cases coincide with references already given in the footnotes to the chapters, in other cases not. They are intended for purposes of general reference to the central themes and topics of this book.

Articles:

Essay, "What (If Anything) to Expect From Today's Philosophers?," **Time,** LXXXVII, No. 1, January 7, 1966, pp. 24-26.

Feuer, L. S., "American Philosophy is Dead," **The New York Times Magazine,** April 24, 1966, pp. 31- 32, p. 122.

Hook, S., "Does Philosophy Have a Future?," **The Saturday Review,** November 11, 1967, pp. 21-22, p. 62.

Kaplan, A., "The Travesty of the Philosophers," **Change in Higher Education,** January-February, 1970, Vol. 2, No. 1-2, pp. 12-19.

Kreyche, R., "Philosophy and The Future of Man," Presidential Address, **American Catholic Philosophical Association Proceedings,** Vol. 42, 1968, pp. 1-9.

Kreyche, R., "Philosophy of Religion: An Introduction," **Akten des XIV. Internationalen Kongresses für philosophie** (Wien), Vol. IV, 1968, pp. 291-295.

Kreyche, R., "The Crisis in American Philosophy and The Spirit of American Youth," **Religion and Society,** Vol. II, No. 6, December, 1969, pp. 10-19.

Kreyche, R., "The Timidity of American Philosophy," **The Center Magazine,** Vol. II, No. 4, July, 1969, p. 29. This is a condensation of remarks that were excerpted from an unpublished address given at the **Center For The Study of Democratic Institutions** on December 28, 1967 at the request of its Director, Dr. Robert Hutchins. The title of the original address is "The Practical Task of Philosophy."

R. Kreyche, "Toward a Recovery of The Dignity of Man," published as a monograph in Phoenix, Ariz. by Southwest Auto Lease, Inc., June, 1968.

Moulds, G. E., "The Decline and Fall of Philosophy," **Liberal Education,** edited by F. L. Warmold, Published by the Association of American Colleges, Vol. I, No. 3, October 1964, pp. 360-364.

Books:

Adler, M., **The Conditions of Philosophy** (New York: Dell Publishing Co, 1967).

Adler, M., **The Idea of Freedom** (Garden City, New York: Doubleday and Co., 1958).

Adler, M., **The Time of Our Lives** (New York: Holt, Rinehart, and Winston, Inc., 1970).

Berdyaev, N., **The Fate of Man in the Modern World** (Ann Arbor: The University of Michigan Press, 1961).

Berdyaev, N., **The Beginning and the End** (New York: Harper & Brothers, 1957).

Boorstin, D., **The Image** (New York: Harper & Row, 1961).

Cole, W. G., **The Restless Quest of Modern Man** (New York: Oxford University Press, 1966).

Dawson, C., **The Historic Reality of Christian Culture** (New York: Harper & Row Publishers, 1965).

De Chardin, P., **The Future of Man,** translated by N. Denny (New York: Harper & Row Publishers, 1964).

Dewey, J., **The Quest for Certainty** (New York: G. P. Putnam's, Inc., 1960).

Dewey, J., **Reconstruction in Philosophy** (Boston: The Beacon Press, 1962).

Dewey, J., **On Experience, Nature, and Freedom** (Indianapolis: The Bobbs-Merrill Co., Inc., 1960).

Dewey, J., **Intelligence in the Modern World** (New York: Random House, 1939).

Heilbroner, R., **The Worldly Philosophers** (New York: Time, Inc., 1962).

James, W., **Pragmatism and Other Essays** (New York: Washington Square Press, 1963).

James, W., **The Varieties of Religious Experience** (New York: The New American Library, 1964).

Kant, I., **Education** (Ann Arbor: The University of Michigan Press, 1960).

Kant, I., **Lectures in Ethics** (New York: Harper & Row Publishers, 1963).

Kaplan, A., **American Ethics and Public Policy** (New York: Oxford University Press, 1963).

Kreyche, R., **First Philosophy** (New York: Holt, Rinehart, and Winston, Inc., 1959).

Kreyche, R., **God and Contemporary Man** (Milwaukee: The Bruce Publishing Co., 1965).

Kreyche, R., **God and Reality** (New York: Holt, Rinehart, and Winston, Inc., 1965).

Lippmann, W., **A Preface to Morals** (Boston: The Beacon Press, 1955).

232

Bibliography

Lippmann, W., **The Public Philosophy** (New York: The New American Library, 1963).

Maritain, J., **Education at the Crossroads** (New Haven: Yale University Press, 1960).

Maritain, J., **Moral Philosophy** (New York: Charles Scribner's Sons, 1964).

Maritain J., **On the Use of Philosophy** (New York: Atheneum, 1965).

Maritain, J., **Reflections on America** (Garden City: Doubleday & Co., Inc., 1958).

Maritain, J., **The Person and The Common Good,** trans. by J. Fitzgerald (Notre Dame, Indiana: University of Notre Dame Press, 1966).

Niebuhr, R., **Moral Man and Immoral Society** (New York: Charles Scribner's Sons, 1932).

Schopenhauer, A., **On the Basis of Morality,** translated by E. Payne (Indianapolis: The Bobbs-Merrill Co., Inc., 1965).

Stern, K., **The Third Revolution** (Garden City: Doubleday & Co., 1954).

Weigel, G., **The Modern God** (New York: The Macmillan Co., 1963).

INDEX